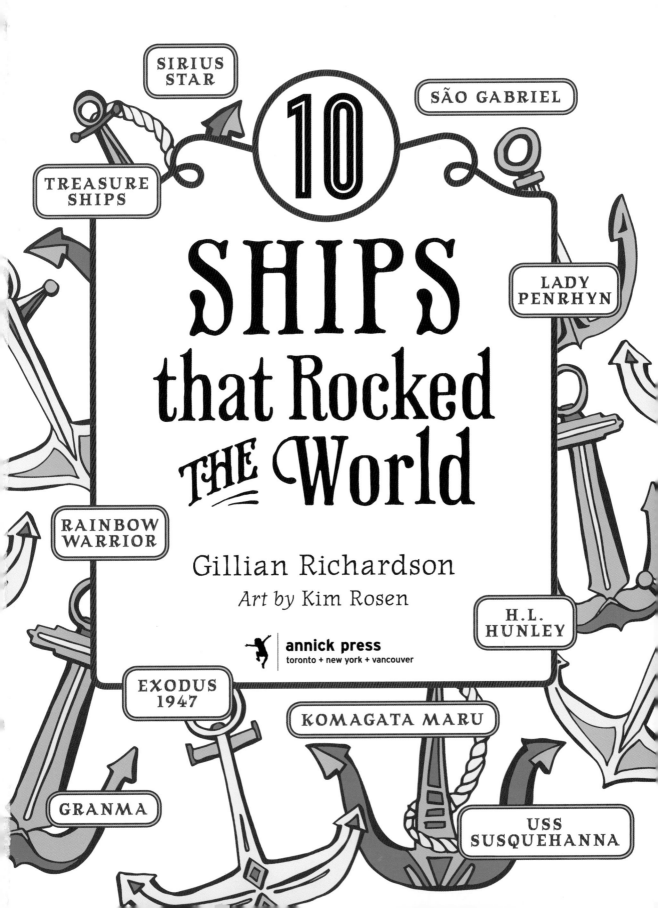

SIRIUS STAR

SÃO GABRIEL

TREASURE SHIPS

10

LADY PENRHYN

SHIPS that Rocked THE World

RAINBOW WARRIOR

Gillian Richardson

Art by Kim Rosen

annick press
toronto + new york + vancouver

H.L. HUNLEY

EXODUS 1947

KOMAGATA MARU

GRANMA

USS SUSQUEHANNA

This one's for you, Dad—G.R.
For Sadie, Emily, Blake, and Dylan—K.R.

Page 168 constitutes an extension of this copyright page.
Edited by Paula Ayer
Proofread by Tanya Trafford
Designed by Natalie Olsen/Kisscut Design

ANNICK PRESS LTD.

We acknowledge the support of the Canada Council for the Arts, the Ontario Arts Council, and the Government of Canada through the Canada Book Fund (CBF) for our publishing activities.

ONTARIO ARTS COUNCIL
CONSEIL DES ARTS DE L'ONTARIO
an Ontario government agency
un organisme du gouvernement de l'Ontario

Cataloging in Publication
Richardson, Gillian, author
10 ships that rocked the world / Gillian Richardson ; art by Kim Rosen.

Includes bibliographical references and index.
Issued in print and electronic formats.
ISBN 978-1-55451-782-4 (bound).—ISBN 978-1-55451-781-7 (pbk.).—
ISBN 978-1-55451-783-1 (html).—ISBN 978-1-55451-784-8 (pdf)

1. Ships—History—Juvenile literature. 2. Boats and boating—History—Juvenile literature. 3. Navigation—History—Juvenile literature. I. Rosen, Kim, 1978–, illustrator II. Title. III. Title: Ten ships that rocked the world.

VM15.R53 2015   j623.82   C2015-900754-2
                                        C2015-900755-0

Published in the U.S.A. by Annick Press (U.S.) Ltd.

Printed in China

Visit us at: www.annickpress.com
Visit Gillian Richardson at: www.books4kids.ca/gillian-richardson
Visit Kim Rosen at: www.kimrosen.com

Also available in e-book format.
Please visit www.annickpress.com/ebooks.html for more details. Or scan

CONTENTS

Introduction

For as long as people have traveled by water, ships have been at the center of their stories. Some ships have even changed the world in surprising ways while sailing through human history.

From earliest times, people used ships to fish, travel, and trade, but because there weren't many good maps or tools for navigation, sailors tended to stay close to their own shores. Beginning in the 15th century, explorers set sail to learn about other cultures, gain wealth from trade, or conquer distant lands. When wars broke out in the 19th and 20th centuries, ships became vital instruments for combat. People displaced by wars often seek a better future in a different land, and even in peacetime they've relied on ships to take them to new homes.

Early exploration by sea helped people understand the world. Zheng He's **TREASURE SHIPS** sailed little-known routes from China

An old ship in port
in Genoa, Italy

at a time when few had traveled so widely. And when explorer Vasco da Gama's **SÃO GABRIEL** set out from Portugal, no one was sure if there was a way into the Indian Ocean around the tip of South Africa. Once travel became more common in the southern Atlantic, England began transporting convicts on ships like the **LADY PENRHYN** to build settlements in Australia. Then, in the 1800s, the United States showed its power at sea, sending the **USS SUSQUEHANNA** to Japan to push for more open communication and trade. Back at home, the embattled American South developed a unique weapon during the Civil War—the submersible **H.L. HUNLEY**—inspiring a new type of warship that made huge impacts in the First and Second World Wars.

The **KOMAGATA MARU** and **EXODUS 1947** both played key roles in helping people seek better and safer lives in new lands. In the 1950s, the **GRANMA** gave passage home to leaders of a revolution that would spark drastic change in a small island nation, and later pose a major threat to global security.

In the 21st century, the world has watched as determined groups of people have used ships to make a big impact. A ship called **RAINBOW WARRIOR** has become a crucial tool in the environmental revolution, while in the impoverished African nation of Somalia, people desperate to make a living sent a jolt through the global economy when they hijacked the oil tanker **SIRIUS STAR**.

Each of these 10 ships caught the world's attention, shining a spotlight on a larger piece of history. Read on to discover how events touched off by these sea journeys have sharpened our understanding of other countries and the people who live there, and of the struggles they've endured. The 10 ships you'll encounter are the source of far-reaching changes that continue to influence the lives of so many.

SHIPS VS. BOATS

What's the difference between a ship and a boat? The answer isn't simple. The term "ship" usually means a seagoing craft, while a boat sails on lakes or rivers. Also, ships are bigger: a ship is big enough to carry a boat. A mariner (sailor) will never call a ship a boat, so the best rule might be to call the ship (or boat) whatever the captain calls it!

1

TREASURE SHIPS

Zheng He's Fabled Fleet

NAME

Chinese treasure ships were large wooden
vessels in the fleet of Admiral Zheng He,
who led seven expeditions in the 1400s.

FUZHOU

COCHI   UTTHAYA

MALDIVES

MOMBASA

BUILT

Beginning in 1403 in Nanjing, China, at seven long dry docks (basins that are pumped dry to allow shipbuilding or repair) next to the Yangtze River. Up to 30,000 workers were involved in their construction, including carpenters, sail and rope makers, and ironsmiths.

DESCRIPTION

Treasure ships were huge—about half as long but almost twice as wide as the *Titanic!* Their astonishing size has been determined by examining pieces found in archaeological digs in the Nanjing dry docks. The fleet also included seven-masted supply ships; six-masted troop ships; five-masted warships; and smaller, faster oared warships, along with tankers carrying fresh water.

CLAIM TO FAME

Columbus, da Gama, Magellan, and... Zheng He? The Chinese explorer might not be as famous as the others, but their fleets were dwarfed by his massive armada of treasure ships. His voyages, stretching from 1405 to 1433, extended China's influence across the Eastern world.

WIDTH: 50 METERS (165 FEET)

LENGTH: 122 METERS (400 FEET)

WHERE ARE THEY NOW?

After their seventh voyage, all the ships were destroyed, along with most plans and records of the journeys.

CHINA [1405]

Tai can barely stand still, so great is his excitement. He's been allowed to journey from his family's farm to the banks of the Yangtze River to be part of the crowd watching the departure of a magnificent fleet of ships. Musicians play, flags wave, people shout and laugh, and the summer sun sparkles off the water. Tai knows the huge ships are special, not just for their size and lavish decorations. He knows this expedition will show China's strength and riches to the world. What an impression the cargo of treasures will make! Of course he's joyful and proud.

But Tai's feelings are mixed. Today he has bid farewell to his father, a soldier sailing with the fleet. Tai might not see him again for two years, or more. As the eldest son, he has been entrusted to look after their farming family in his father's absence. He hopes he will be worthy of that trust.

Tai wishes he were old enough to go on the expedition too. He admires the great commander Zheng He for his courage and skill. What he wouldn't give to see the fabled lands he's heard stories about, to talk with their people and learn about their cultures! As he watches the ships set sail, he vows to work hard at the farming skills his father has taught him. Maybe there will be more expeditions, and Tai can be a soldier on one of those ships someday.

The Story of the Treasure Ships

WHERE CHINA'S YANGTZE RIVER FLOWS into the Pacific Ocean, an armada of 317 awe-inspiring ships, some of the largest and most elaborate ever built, proudly raised their sails and set out to sea. The year was 1405. Over the next 30 years, Commander Zheng He would lead six more expeditions, giving China authority over the Southeast Asian region. But the aim of these voyages was not to invade or conquer countries. Rather, China intended to show off the empire's extreme wealth, intelligence, and power. These grand adventures would leave a profound impression on the 15th-century world. But what inspired them in the first place?

China's Ties to the Sea

RECORDS OF CHINA'S HISTORY dating back to 1600 BCE show times of both war and peace with its neighbors. Because much of the country is bordered by ocean, deserts, and mountains, its leaders could choose how much contact to have with the outside world. Goods and ideas were exchanged with lands to the west over a difficult overland trading route called the Silk Road. But China was a seafaring nation, so its merchants also sailed to trading posts throughout Indonesia and India.

Many dynasties—kings or emperors belonging to the same family—have ruled China. In the late 13th century, aggressive northern invaders called Mongols, led by Kublai Khan, seized power. Eventually, though, the Mongol tribes were driven out, and the Ming dynasty (1368–1644) began to bring new order and economic prosperity to the country. Zhu Di, the third Ming emperor, wanted other countries to recognize China's superiority and magnificence. He planned to expand the country's trade by sea and bring back a traditional system called *tribute*. As part of the plan, China would show off its expertise in shipbuilding and sailing with a series of expeditions to Southeast Asian countries.

Emperor Zhu Di

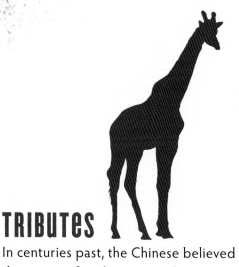

TRIBUTES

In centuries past, the Chinese believed their country was the center of civilization, and its emperor a supreme power whose authority came straight from heaven. So if other countries wanted to trade for China's wealth of silk, gold, and other luxuries, they first had to "pay tribute" to show their high regard for China's power. The tribute might be special gifts unique to their region, like the zebras and giraffes ambassadors brought from Africa. Gifts were respectfully presented by performing *kowtow*—kneeling and bowing the head to the floor. In return, the Chinese emperor would give valuables, permission to trade with China, and the promise of China's military protection if needed. Both sides gained: the traders got the goods they wanted, and China's position in the world was continuously strengthened. During the Ming dynasty, more than 100 countries sent ambassadors with tributes for the emperor.

A Bold Plan with a Bold Leader

SOME DISAPPROVED OF Zhu Di's grand plans. Confucians, a powerful group that believed peace and harmony were all-important, feared too much foreign trade would unsettle the country. But the emperor's ambition could not be crushed. He chose his trusted general, Zheng He, to command the fleet. As a Muslim, Zheng He's knowledge of the Islamic religion and Arabic languages would help him convince foreigners that a close trading connection with China, the world's most powerful empire, was a good idea.

CONFUCIANISM

Confucius (551–479 BCE) was a philosopher whose ideas strongly influenced thought in China for over 2,000 years. Confucianism is based in peace and harmony and teaches that everyone should know his or her proper place. Rulers must be powerful but honorable and guide their people in a calm manner. They are accountable to heaven if their conduct is not correct.

Similarly, families were expected to work within the rules of their community and show consideration for the needs of others.

For instance, parents should protect their children, and a person should do his job well since his performance will reflect upon his family's good name.

The Voyage Begins

Ocean winds ballooned the fleet's massive, brilliantly colored sails on that July day in 1405. As far as the eye could see, ships rode the waves, their bows pointed south along China's coast. Their destinations? Zheng He would spread his emperor's message of peace and order to Vietnam, then west to Siam (now Thailand), Malacca (in Malaysia), and Sumatra (in Indonesia). He would offer extravagant gifts to Ceylon (now Sri Lanka) and Malabar, India. Among the riches were silk and porcelain, cotton, tea, fragrant oils, and majestic ceremonial clothing embroidered with dragons—the ancient Chinese symbol of power, representing the emperor. These treasures would be exchanged for tributes of precious tropical spices and foods, ivory, pearls, rare fragrant woods, exotic animals, textiles, and minerals, as well as other goods that China didn't have.

The fleet would cover around 6,000 kilometers (3,726 miles)—about the distance from New York to London—and would not return home for two years.

A puppet show depicting Zheng He

No Ships to Compare

AMONG THE 317 VESSELS in Zheng He's first fleet were at least four massive treasure ships, believed to be the largest ever built completely of wood. Unique Chinese craftsmanship meant there was no need for the iron supports normally used to strengthen such huge vessels. On each ship, 12 square red silk sails on 9 masts, staggered on several levels of decks, captured the wind efficiently. Enormous anchors on either side helped to steady the cumbersome ship. It was a marvel of originality for its rudder (a flat piece of wood at the back of a ship that is moved to change the vessel's direction), which could be raised if the ship sailed close to shore and lowered again in deeper water, and for its double hull (the bottom and sides of the ship), with water-tight compartments to protect the valuables stowed inside.

A wall relief near the ships' building site in Nanjing

BURIED TREASURE

Since most records of the treasure ships were destroyed long ago, how do we know their size? In 1962, a rudder was dug up during excavations of the dry docks in Nanjing where the ships were apparently built. Archaeologists believe that at 11 meters (36 feet) long, it had to have been made for a ship over 122 meters (400 feet) in length.

Treasure ship
replica in Nanjing

That kind of engineering wasn't seen in Europe until almost 400 years later. For a show of power, the ships carried 24 cast-bronze cannons, each with a firing range of about three city blocks.

The passengers—Ming dynasty officials, foreign-language translators, astronomers to study the stars for navigation, physicians, and others—sailed in regal style. Luxurious cabins opened onto hallways lined with windows and balconies. The prow (the front of the boat) had carved animal heads and dragon eyes to "guide" the fleet. The stern (the back of the boat) was decorated with symbolic dragon, phoenix, or eagle designs. The ships were brightly painted, with the bottom whitewashed up to a red waterline (where the surface of the water touches the side). Above that, a pattern of suns and moons circled the hull. Imagine seeing these incredible ships sailing toward you! You couldn't help but feel awe for the empire that displayed such splendor.

Taking Care of Every Need

Many smaller supply vessels accompanied the treasure ships, carrying horses, tools, and materials to repair ships at sea, and food for an astounding crew of 28,000 seamen and workmen. Since the expedition might not touch land for weeks at a time, tanker ships carried fresh water to transfer to other ships while at sea. Navigators used compasses (invented in China, and first used around 1100 CE) and star maps to chart their course over the southern oceans.

Ships kept contact with each other using bells, drums, or gongs. Information could also be shared by using banners, flags, lanterns, or even carrier pigeons. Troop ships had soldiers on board. A number of smaller, faster warships could put the run to pirates with cannons that used gunpowder (invented in China around 900 CE). This show of force was only meant to discourage conflict, though, as Zheng He's primary mission was peaceful contact.

Pirates and Peace

But huge ships carrying such wealth tempted bold pirates like Chen Zuyi, who had long prowled the narrow Strait of Malacca. He was one of the most feared pirates in the region, with 10 ships and thousands of men in his command, but met a costly end after pretending to surrender to Zheng He while actually preparing an attack. The story goes that a local spy revealed the foolish trick to Zheng He, and in the resulting battle, 5000 pirates were killed. Chen Zuyi was captured and held for execution back in China. The spy, on the other hand, was well rewarded for his loyalty to the emperor. He became the new ruler of the former pirate-controlled city of

HOW DO WE KNOW ABOUT ZHENG HE?

Few written records of Zheng He's accomplishments exist today. But details about this legendary maritime adventurer remain on three stone tablets engraved with his thoughts. One was created on the eve of the first expedition, in 1405, and placed at Kunyang (now in Korea), at the grave of his father. Its words express Zheng He's admiration for the qualities of humility and charity toward others. A second monument, near Galle, Sri Lanka, bears a plea to figures from three different religions—Buddha (the founder of Buddhism), Shiva (a Hindu god), and Allah (the Muslim name for God)—for their protective blessing for the voyages. Historians have pointed to it as a rare show of tolerance for different religions at a time when followers of those religions were likely to hold hostile attitudes toward one another. The third stone, at Changle, China, is engraved with Zheng He's description of the purpose of his voyages to "more than 30 countries large and small."

Statues of Zheng He, like this one in Indonesia, are found across Southeast Asia.

Palembang, on Sumatra, which was given military protection and special trading rights with China.

Besides establishing peaceful relations with other countries, Zheng He's voyages were also intended to help create order in the region, as the Ming emperor was doing with his policies at home. In Ceylon, during the third expedition, Zheng He's soldiers were able to control the fighting between the Hindu Tamils and Sinhalese Buddhists. There was no lasting peace, though: unresolved divisions remain between those groups in today's Sri Lanka.

Venturing Westward

The FIFTH VOYAGE, IN 1417, took Zheng He to the coast of Africa, possibly as far south as what's now Somalia, Kenya, and Mozambique. China and Africa had long been trading partners—archaeologists have found pieces of Chinese pottery dating from the first century CE along the African coast. But how Zheng He must have marveled at the strange animals—giraffes, zebras, and ostriches! He invited African ambassadors to bring them to China as tributes, along with priceless elephant ivory and rhinoceros horn (to be used as medicine). On later voyages, he returned those ambassadors to their homes and explored more of the coast. Had he been sailing 70 years later, he might have met the Portuguese explorer Vasco da Gama on his first foray around the tip of South Africa.

Islam was the predominant religion throughout the regions Zheng He visited in the 15th century. His Muslim father had made the traditional pilgrimage, or hajj, to Mecca, where Muslims gather to show Islam's central virtue of humility. But Zheng He now owed his loyalty to the Chinese emperor and couldn't worship at that holy shrine himself. However, on his seventh and final voyage, to the Arabian Peninsula and the Red Sea, Zheng He sent a delegation to visit Mecca. He died in 1433 on the return voyage and is believed to have been buried at sea.

China's Legacy to the World

AFTER ZHENG HE'S EXPEDITIONS, great change came about in China. The conservative political forces of Confucianism overruled the next Ming emperor and the lavish, costly ocean journeys ended. As had happened many times before, China turned its back on the world, even banning overseas trade and giving up its power on the sea. The country's dislike for outside influences became so strong that most records of the voyages were destroyed and the great ships were burned.

The voyages of the treasure fleet were unique in many ways. Besides the fact that China had the largest ships in the world and a massive armada, it took a remarkable understanding of technology, science, and sheer sailing know-how to navigate the largely unknown waters. The fleet covered impressive distances, and the Chinese shared their sailing skills with many other countries, along with their knowledge of farming, medicine, and architecture. In return, ambassadors from other countries taught the Chinese about their customs and culture. This amazing exchange of ideas came during one of the country's most productive eras. In contrast, European countries didn't begin expanding their empires through exploration for close to another 100 years.

HONORING THE PAST

In 2005, China marked the 600th anniversary of Zheng He's first expedition with celebrations throughout the country and a lavish exhibit at the National Museum in Beijing. Chinese officials hoped the exhibit would show the world how Zheng He's voyages had inspired peaceful trade rather than conquest, as well as proving that his achievements equaled those of more famous explorers like Columbus and Magellan. Seven years later, construction began on a model of one of Zheng He's treasure ships, using archaeological evidence found during excavations in the Nanjing shipyard. The replica ship was intended to be ready for sea trials by 2014, but a shortage of funds has delayed the project.

A 2005 stamp commemorates the 600th anniversary of Zheng He's first voyage.

2

SÃO GABRIEL

A New Route to India

NAME

For Saint Gabriel, a Biblical messenger
from God. Gabriel's image was carved as
the figurehead on the ship's prow.

LISBON

CALICUT

MOSSEL BAY

DESCRIPTION

The ship's design, called a *carrack* or *nao* (both words meaning ship), was a combination of Mediterranean and Northern European styles. This stable vessel could carry trade goods and enough men and food for long journeys, making it a favorite of Portuguese explorers. It had a wide, deep hull with higher fore (front) and aft (rear) sections, and a rounded stern. Three masts carried a combination of square and lateen (triangular) sails. It had 20 guns for defense.

BUILT

In 1497, under the supervision of Bartolomeu Dias

DRAFT (DISTANCE BETWEEN WATERLINE AND BOTTOM OF HULL): 2.3 METERS (7.5 FEET)

WIDTH: 8.5 METERS (28 FEET)

LENGTH: 25.7 METERS (84 FEET)

CLAIM TO FAME

In 1497, the *São Gabriel*, commanded by explorer Vasco da Gama, sailed from Lisbon, Portugal, to India. Da Gama was the first to link Europe and India by sea around the southern tip of Africa, opening up the route to trade and exploration.

WHERE IS IT NOW?

The ship, only serving until 1499, completed just one voyage. Its eventual fate is unknown.

OFF AFRICA'S EASTERN COAST [1497]

"Ahoy! There it is!"

The shout comes from a sailor clinging high up São Gabriel's mast. Tomaas follows the direction of the man's outstretched arm, pointing toward the shore. He strains to see the tall stone cross they've been anxiously watching for, built by Bartolomeu Dias nine years earlier. Standing atop a rocky outcrop above the beach, it's the sign they have reached the northern limit of the Dias expedition.

Tomaas feels a shiver down his back. From this point on, they will be in unknown waters. No other explorers have passed this way at sea. Who knows what dangers lurk ahead? That same fear, and the fact that they were short of food, had driven Dias's crew to threaten mutiny if their captain didn't return to Portugal. But Tomaas knows his captain, da Gama, is convinced that this is the sea route to India. After sailing through the extreme winds around the Cape of Good Hope, they are now in warmer, calmer Indian Ocean waters. There will be no turning back.

It was good to spend the past few days ashore, trading trinkets with the natives for much-needed food. Before they left, Tomaas and the rest of the crew had burned the supply ship, damaged in storms at the Cape. Now with their small fleet of three ships more tightly packed, they must find the riches that lie ahead—spices, precious gems, and gold—to take home to Portugal.

Tomaas takes a last look at the stone cross, says a silent prayer, then turns his eyes to the north.

The Story of the São Gabriel

IF YOU PLANNED TO SAIL THE OCEAN, would you go without taking a GPS device along? You'd want the latest charts and weather information at your fingertips, and a way to communicate with home. You'd take fresh water and dried food that would store easily and keep well. But at one time, sailors had to do without such modern technology and conveniences, or even accurate knowledge of what to expect on a long journey at sea. Five hundred years ago, aboard his sailing ship *São Gabriel*, the Portuguese explorer Vasco da Gama braved unknown seas. His voyage to India would not only transform the world's understanding of its oceans, but also turn the dream of finding a new trade route to a secret land of riches into reality.

What Early Sailors Knew

Europeans had not ventured far into the Atlantic Ocean in the early 1400s. Around the Mediterranean Sea they welcomed trade goods brought overland from East Asia, or from Arab sea traders. On the western edge of Europe, though, Portugal's merchants grew tired of paying extra transport costs for Eastern luxuries. Was there a way to reach the source of those goods by sea? Could Portuguese traders make huge profits by shipping highly valued spices themselves? In the late 15th century, Henry the Navigator, an explorer and son of the Portuguese king, encouraged the search for new sea routes along the Atlantic coast of Africa. He even established a school for navigators, mapmakers, and astronomers.

As ship designs and navigational tools improved, so did the confidence of sailors. Many myths and fears existed about the unknown waters to the west. Sailors told stories of sea monsters and boiling tropical oceans. More realistically, they worried that the North Star—their trusted means of direction-finding—could no longer be seen once they sailed south of the equator (the imaginary line around the Earth that is the same distance from the North and South poles). Eventually they overcame those fears: the lure of riches known to come from India was too strong. If the Portuguese didn't get a move on, Spain, Britain, and France might beat them to India and the wealth it held.

WHAT IS GPS?

The Global Positioning System (GPS) is a navigation system developed in 1973. Timed signals from satellites in space picked up on a GPS device will show one's location anywhere on Earth.

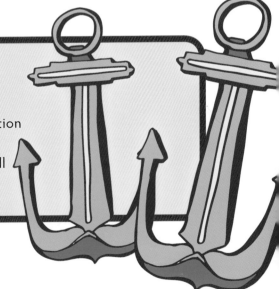

A Key Discovery

PORTUGAL DID NOT KNOW the exact locations of the best spice ports in India. Muslim traders with a long-standing dislike of Christians controlled all the known routes to that area. But finding a sea route around Africa would allow traders to sail directly into Indian ports. In 1487, when a storm unexpectedly took the Portuguese explorer Bartolomeu Dias around the tip of Africa, he found himself sailing on its east coast. Before that, some had believed that Africa was joined to another southern continent (which we now know as Antarctica). Here was absolute proof that it wasn't. Dias turned back after coming across unfriendly aboriginals at Mossel Bay (just east of today's Cape Town) and running low on food. But he knew the long-desired sea route to the east—to India—lay ahead. Could Portugal be the first to reach its riches?

This map from 1500 shows how Europeans pictured Africa after da Gama's discoveries.

THE ORDER OF CHRIST

The huge square sails of the *São Gabriel* and *São Rafael* were decorated with a red cross, symbol of the Order of Christ. This military group's main mission was to fight against Muslims, seen as enemies by the Christian king of Portugal.

The Voyage Begins

COMMANDING A FLEET OF FOUR SHIPS from the *São Gabriel*, Vasco da Gama left Lisbon on July 8, 1497. His flagship, and the *São Rafael*, with his brother Paulo as captain, each had a deep hull so huge cargos of spices and other valuables could be brought home from India. Square and lateen sails allowed for speed and ease of steering. A smaller caravel (sailing ship), called the *Berrio*, and a supply ship completed the armada.

Out in the Atlantic past the Spanish-owned Canary Islands, the ships struggled to stay together in the fog. They spent a week in the Cape Verde islands, a Portuguese colony off Africa's west coast, doing repairs and taking on fresh water and meat. The Doldrums—an area of alternately calm and stormy waters near the equator—tested their endurance for days. Then, to avoid treacherous winds and currents known to occur near Africa's coast, da Gama pushed farther to the west before turning south. In this new and mysterious region

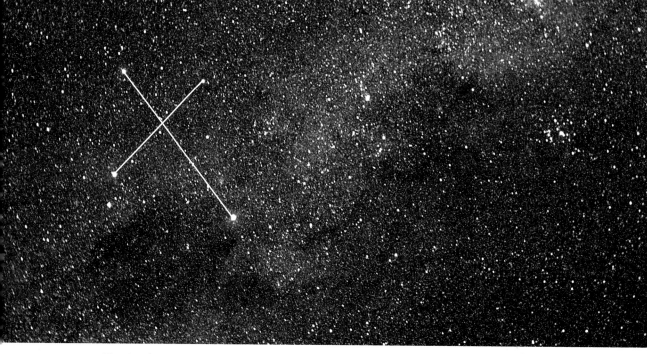

The Southern Cross constellation

across the equator, the sailors had to rely on stars of the Southern Cross to guide them. They calculated their position with an astrolabe—an instrument that measures the height of the sun—and a compass. Da Gama hoped to fill his huge square sails with the strong westerly winds that had blown Dias's ships toward South Africa. The gamble paid off, but only after 93 days with no sight of land.

SOUTHERN CROSS

A constellation called the Southern Cross is named for the shape created if imaginary vertical and horizontal lines were to link its four stars. The vertical line points roughly to the sky above the South Pole. Visible south of the equator, the Southern Cross can be used as a navigational aid, much like the North Star in the northern hemisphere.

15TH-CENTURY NAVIGATIONAL TOOLS

COMPASS: Invented in China and seen in Europe by the 1100s, it is used for finding directions in relation to north as a starting point.

MARINER'S ASTROLABE: An instrument used to find a vessel's latitude—the distance north or south of the equator—by measuring the height of the sun above the horizon at exactly midday.

LEAD LINE: Possibly the oldest navigational tool, dating from ancient Egyptian times, this lead weight on a rope marked at regular intervals alerts the crew to shallow waters to prevent running the ship aground.

DEAD RECKONING: A method of calculating one's position by starting with a known position and measuring speed over time in a known direction.

A mariner's astrolabe

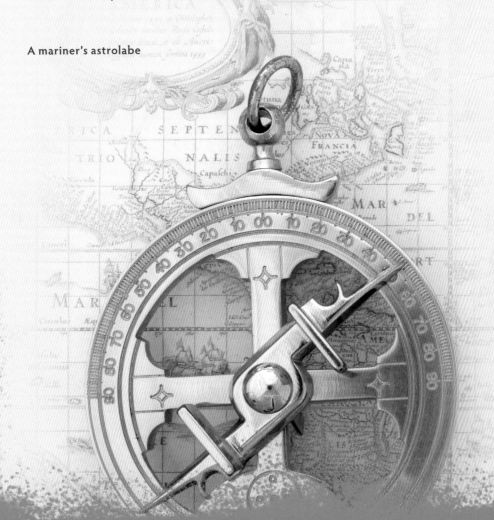

Making Contact in Africa

Anxious to replenish supplies of fresh water and food, da Gama anchored in a bay near the Cape of Good Hope at the southern tip of Africa. The first aboriginal people he met had little to trade, so the fleet moved on. It battled fierce winds around the Cape and the supply ship suffered damage. Landing on Africa's east coast, the sailors encountered many aboriginals who appeared interested in making trades for food. But when the crews took fresh water without asking, they were chased off.

Da Gama had decided to burn his battered supply ship, so only three ships sailed north, past the point where Dias had turned back. With no more charts to follow on this unmapped coast, da Gama named some of the new lands, such as the Natal area (in what's now South Africa), where they landed at Christmas. At another stop on the Quelimane River (in today's Mozambique), friendly people greeted them and provided food and water. The fleet rested there for a month, and da Gama learned that some of the locals had seen large ships like his before. That meant they must be getting closer to the desired trading routes. But after so many months at sea, the crew began to show signs of scurvy and about 30 of them died.

They continued to sail farther north. At the Muslim city-state of Mozambique, da Gama must have been excited to see Arab ships loaded with spices, gold, and jewels from the East. But he realized these traders controlled this coast, so he cautiously let everyone onshore think his party was also Muslim. He paid a visit to the ruler of Mozambique, who was insulted by the trivial gifts da Gama offered in exchange for highly valued spices. So it was not surprising that hostilities broke out when the Muslim ruler discovered that these foreigners were actually Christians. Eventually da Gama's ships were driven off without the guides they'd hoped would take them across the difficult waters of the Indian Ocean.

They say bad news travels fast! The Portuguese were not well received in Mombasa (a port city in Kenya) either, since the sultan there had heard of the trouble in Mozambique. Forced to continue sailing north, da Gama finally found a friendlier reception at the next port, Malindi. It seemed that Mombasa and Malindi were at war, and even Christian allies were welcomed. The Portuguese would later establish a trading post at Malindi. But da Gama had a more urgent goal, and he set sail—this time with a Christian guide—for India. Good luck for a change! The southwesterly monsoon winds blew them to India in only 23 days.

USING MONSOONS TO ADVANTAGE

Monsoon (Arabic for "season" or "weather") winds of Southeast Asia change direction over the Indian Ocean from summer to winter. They rush toward the subcontinent of India to fill the low-pressure area left when summer heat rises from the land. Loaded with moisture, the winds are forced upward by the Himalayan mountains and dump torrential rain in the region. In fall, cooler, drier air plunges down from the mountains and over the ocean. For thousands of years, Arab traders used the southwest monsoon winds as the speediest way to get to India's coast, then let the northeast wind push them home to the Arabian Peninsula with their cargos of spices.

FOOD FOR a LONG VOYAGE

Early sailors had few effective ways to keep food fresh on long journeys at sea. So they took things like hardtack (a cracker), salt beef or pork, dried cod, and cheese. Beans, flour, and onions would keep for a while, but fresh fruits and vegetables would not, especially in hot, humid climates. The only food available far from land and guaranteed to be fresh was fish! It was cooked with olive oil, and often eaten with rice. The most common beverage of the day was wine, as fresh water failed to stay drinkable for long in wooden barrels, especially in hot climates where algae and bacteria would soon start to grow. In the 1400s, little was known about the dreaded weakening disease scurvy. It is caused by lack of vitamin C, but early sailors had no idea which foods would prevent it. And even though it is made from fruit, wine was no help, as the vitamin C in wine grapes is lost as they ripen.

A painting from 1900 depicts locals in Calicut watching da Gama's arrival.

Not Welcome!

Aᴛ ꜰɪʀꜱᴛ ᴅᴀ Gᴀᴍᴀ ꜰᴇʟᴛ ᴡᴇʟᴄᴏᴍᴇ in Calicut, famed center of the spice trade. Hindus (whom da Gama mistook for Christians) controlled the city and its vast storehouses. Muslim traders brought in silk, jewels, and porcelain from China, highly prized pepper from India, and cinnamon and cloves from a group of islands in Indonesia known as the Moluccas, or Spice Islands. These two religious groups—Muslims and Hindus—held vastly different beliefs and only worked side by side for mutual profit.

The wealthy Hindu ruler, the Zamorin, expected gifts of gold in return for spices. Again, da Gama had no such riches to offer. In fact, he was unable to make any significant trades during his three months in Calicut. When news of the earlier skirmishes reached India, the Portuguese were branded as liars and pirates. Muslim traders were convinced they threatened to cut into their profits.

No more friendly dealings! Da Gama's three ships had to fight their way out of port with barely enough supplies for the journey home, and only a few samplings of spices. To make matters worse, powerful August monsoon winds worked against them. The voyage back to Malindi took four times longer than the spring crossing, and more of the crew fell victim to scurvy. At last, with barely enough hands left to sail the *São Gabriel* and the *Berrio*, da Gama deliberately sank the *São Rafael* and headed home. Of the 170 men who had set out 732 days earlier, only 54 made it back to Portugal. Da Gama's brother was not among them; he had died on the way home.

NOT SO SHIP-SHAPE

Wooden ships like the *São Gabriel* did not hold up well to long voyages. They leaked and collected so many barnacles and weeds that the hull had to be regularly scraped (called *careening*) and resealed. In warm tropical waters, worms that burrowed into the wood were a particular problem, causing extensive leakage. Wooden spars broke, sails tore, and ropes wore out. During months at sea, the wood took on a foul odor from garbage, dirty bilge water, and lack of sanitation. Pests, including rats, cockroaches, and fleas, multiplied on board, and the likelihood of disease outbreaks grew.

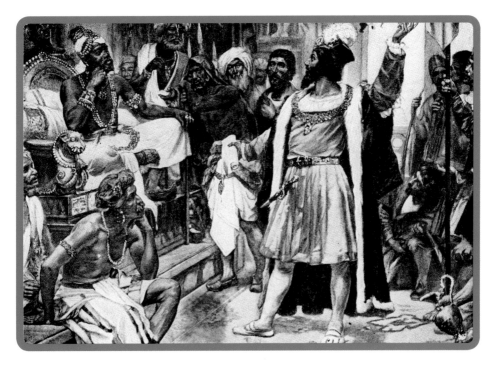

Leaving a Bad Impression

ALTHOUGH HIS FIRST ENCOUNTER with traders in India was not profitable in terms of merchandise, da Gama had proved that a sea route from Europe existed around Africa. The way was clear not only to secure trade routes, but also to spread the Christian religion: both had been major objectives of Portugal's king.

The Portuguese returned twice to India, in 1500 and 1502, with revenge in mind. They raided, looted, and killed Muslims and Hindus, and sometimes destroyed entire cities when they met with anti-Portuguese reactions. Da Gama even captured a ship full of defenseless pilgrims returning from worshipping at Mecca, and savagely tortured and murdered them. Portugal eventually seized the power it craved over Indian Ocean trade routes and ports, but the country made many enemies in the process. Predictably, in 1524,

Da Gama was featured on this Portuguese stamp from 1969.

when da Gama was sent to India as viceroy, his mission to build a better relationship between Portugal and India was doomed from the start. He died there later that year. While he still holds a place of high honor in Portugal for his contributions to the country's trade and prosperity, da Gama is viewed to this day with hatred and anger by many Indians and Africans.

Opening the Way for Others

BY REALIZING THEIR DREAM of reaching the Indian Ocean, the Portuguese gained valuable knowledge. They discovered the sources of spices sold at Mediterranean markets and how traders determined their prices. They learned about different cultures and ancient conflicts at play between religious groups. Perhaps most importantly, da Gama's appearance in India ended the Arab traders' monopoly on the region. In Europe, it meant that more and more trade goods would arrive through the sea port of Lisbon. Portuguese ships pushed even farther eastward by 1513 to trade with China and Japan. After the Portuguese, the British and Dutch challenged each other for a share of the trading scene in the 16th century. This profitable world of Eastern trade was soon opened to all.

The successful voyage of the *São Gabriel* has been called one of the greatest ocean expeditions in history. Besides revealing the sea passage to India, da Gama and his crew learned how the South Atlantic winds worked. Portuguese mapmakers created highly accurate early maps, showing land outlines and sea routes that would help other explorers. The Portuguese would soon claim Brazil, and on an expedition from 1519 to 1522, explorer Ferdinand Magellan would be the first to sail west from Europe around the tip of South America and across the Pacific Ocean to Asia. Although Magellan died in the Philippines, his ships completed the voyage around the globe. Building on the *São Gabriel*'s achievements, Portugal remained a powerful empire for 600 years.

The Monument to the Discoveries in Lisbon, Portugal, celebrates the accomplishments of da Gama and other early navigators.

3

LADY PENRHYN

Exiled to Australia

NAME
For Lady Ann Susannah, wife of
Baron Penrhyn of Ireland

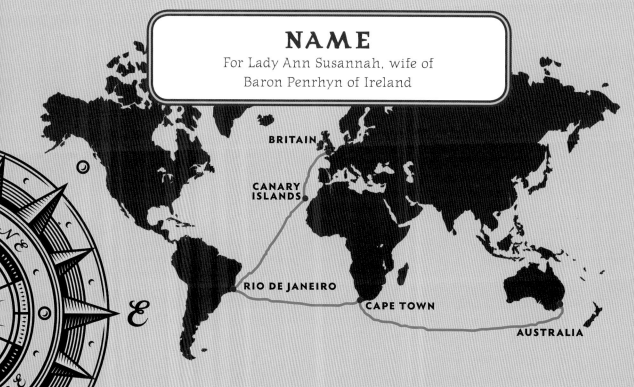

BRITAIN

CANARY
ISLANDS

RIO DE JANEIRO

CAPE TOWN

AUSTRALIA

BUILT
On the Thames
River, London, 1786

DESCRIPTION
Three-masted cargo vessel

CLAIM TO FAME
Lady Penrhyn sailed to Australia
on an eight-month voyage in 1787
carrying 104 female convicts—
the first of 165,000 people who
would be exiled to Australia from
Britain over the next 80 years.

WIDTH:
8.4 METERS
(27.5 FEET)

WEIGHT:
338 TONS

LENGTH: 31.6 METERS (104 FEET)

WHERE IS IT NOW?
After sailing to China for tea in 1788 under charter to the East
India Company, then back to England in 1789, *Lady Penrhyn*
was sold for cargo runs between London and Jamaica.
It was burned and scuttled (or sunk) in Grenada in 1811.

SHEFFIELD, ENGLAND [1780]

Mary hides in the early-morning shadows of an alley watching the activity in the market square. She hopes no one will notice her as she waits for her chance. If a few more people gather on the street, she'll be able to slip out among the crowd and get close enough to the baker's stall. But it's hard to be patient when her stomach growls constantly with hunger.

If only she had a penny to buy an oatcake. Then she wouldn't have to steal it. One oatcake will be barely enough to share with her little brother and her mother, although Mum hardly eats anything since she became too sick to look for work. It's now up to Mary to keep them fed somehow—even if she has to risk getting caught stealing.

Her fingers itch and her heart pounds. Dash in, grab the oatcake and run, hiding it under her shawl. Like her friend Grace had done last week. Only Grace had been caught taking a few potatoes. Mary remembers her friend's terrified look as the police dragged her away to jail. And she hasn't seen Grace since. She's heard that another carriage full of young women has been taken south to London, to Newgate Prison. If that rumor is true, she'll never see Grace again. Once you're in Newgate, you probably won't ever get out, even for such a minor crime. Death is more certain. Or Transportation—people have disappeared on ships sent to Australia, half a world away. Whatever would her mother and brother do if that happened to Mary?

She wrings her hands. Steal the oatcake and risk prison, or starve? What choice does she have?

The Story of the Lady Penrhyn

I F YOU STOLE A T-SHIRT FROM A STORE, you'd expect to face
consequences. You might be made to pay a fine or spend time doing
community service or in detention. You probably wouldn't expect to
be sent far away forever or—hard to even imagine—executed. But that's
exactly the kind of punishment your crime of shoplifting might have
received in 18th-century England.

Locked in the dark, cramped hold of the *Lady Penrhyn*, a three-
masted wooden ship that set sail on May 13, 1787, were convicts facing
sentences of 7 years, or 14 years, or life. Of course, some were hardened
criminals who had committed violent crimes. But most were only
guilty of being poor, homeless, and uneducated. For the theft of a

few yards of printed cotton or six teaspoons, or for poaching a fish from a park pond—anything to eat or sell to keep body and soul together—they now knew they'd never see their home country or their families again. Why were they being banished for the rest of their days to Australia, a remote land they knew nothing about?

Cruel Consequences

TRANSPORTATION, as this harsh punishment was called, was an answer to a problem that arose as the Industrial Revolution drew people from farms to cities, and machines took away jobs. While some people grew rich, those without a way of earning money for food, clothing, or shelter turned to theft as they struggled to survive. If arrested, most ended up in the filthy, overcrowded cells of London's Newgate Prison, awaiting their sentences.

Flogging (being beaten with a whip or rope) or hanging were common penalties. And since the 1600s, England had also sold many convicts as workers to merchants in America. In 1783, after the American colonies won their independence from England in the American Revolution, those convicts were no longer welcome. Where could they be sent, then?

The British government had its eye on Botany Bay—on the other side of the world. When the explorer James Cook visited the continent we now call Australia, in 1770, he claimed its east coast, including Botany Bay, for England. Based on Cook's report of a fair climate, good soil, and a lack of hostile animals or indigenous people, the government decided to set up a penal colony there, and get the convicts to do the work. It was an expensive option, at about 30 pounds (about 300 US dollars today) per convict. But it would relieve the overcrowded prison system and at the same time firmly establish possession of this new territory, which had the advantage of being close to trade routes to China.

Life Aboard a Convict Ship

BEGINNING IN 1783, the *Lady Penrhyn* was one of 11 "First Fleet" ships fitted out to carry convicts to Australia. These unfortunate souls had been living in dreadful conditions in Newgate Prison or on run-down warships called hulks. Of the nearly 1,500 convicts who made the journey aboard the 11 vessels, more than half were first-time offenders, and only a fraction had committed brutal crimes. The majority were men, but only female prisoners—104 women and 8 children—would sail on the *Lady Penrhyn*.

On board the ship, the convicts were locked into the lowest cargo deck each night. The low ceiling made it impossible to stand upright. Ankle chains secured them to narrow sleeping bunks or hammocks. Thin, ragged clothing and one blanket per person barely protected them from the constant cold and dampness. Woolen clothing would have kept them warmer, but it was known to harbor itchy lice (later proven to be the cause of a deadly disease, typhus). Toilets were buckets covered by a board with holes, and not always emptied regularly. There was no privacy and so little ventilation in the hold that it grew revoltingly smelly from unwashed bodies, human waste, and seasickness. The ship's hospital had only one surgeon to handle illness and injuries. Adding to the discomfort was the noise of so many crammed into such a tight space—imagine living with 120 others in a space about the size of a tennis court.

PRISON HULKS

Transportation didn't stop overcrowding in England's prison hulks, the old ships that were moored in rivers near large cities, and were still in use until 1853. Among them, for 25 years, was HMS *Discovery*, the ship in which Captain George Vancouver had explored the Pacific in the 1790s.

As bad as this home would be for the next eight months, convicts at sea were somewhat better off than they had been in prison. Captain Arthur Phillip, who commanded the fleet and would become the first governor of the colony, insisted the convicts on each ship be allowed on deck during the day for fresh air and exercise. After all, the workforce had to be strong enough upon arrival in Australia to build the new colony. For the safety of all, a barrier topped with iron spikes separated convicts and crew, and armed guards were placed at hatchways that opened onto the deck. Food—gruel (like porridge) for breakfast and meat stew with bread at midday—was cooked in a galley, or kitchen, area on deck. These regular meals were a decided improvement over the convicts' skimpy prison rations of thin soup and moldy biscuits. Supplies such as gardening tools and seeds, and building materials needed to construct the settlement, filled some of the deck space.

Long Weeks at Sea

SEASICKNESS PLAGUED the *Lady Penrhyn* in the first days. Its queasy passengers got some relief in the Canary Islands off Africa's northwest coast, the first of several stops for fresh water and provisions, since without refrigeration, food spoiled quickly. This problem grew worse when they were becalmed further south in the Doldrums; the space below decks became increasingly hot and stuffy.

Underway again, the ships crossed the equator on July 14. Following an old tradition of paying tribute to the mythical King Neptune, god of the sea, anyone "crossing the line" for the first time had to participate in rituals including being dunked in water, or playing embarrassing roles in a skit. On the *Lady Penrhyn*, the boisterous fun distracted the crew and almost led to a collision with another vessel. The hot tropical seas brought an unwelcome order from the captain to reduce the daily ration of water to 3 pints

The light blue color of the turbulent Cook Strait—between New Zealand's North and South Islands—indicates sediment stirred up by Roaring Forties winds.

DOLDRUMS AND ROARING FORTIES

The Doldrums are areas in the Atlantic and Pacific oceans near the equator. Rising warm air creates little or no wind and can slow the progress of ships under sail, sometimes for weeks. (You might have heard someone described as being "down in the doldrums"—it means they're depressed or inactive.) In contrast, the Roaring Forties, farther south, often carry hurricane-force winds, some of the strongest on Earth. These notorious westerlies (winds are named for the direction from which they blow) occur when tropical air that rises over the Doldrums moves toward the South Pole. Sinking back down around the fortieth latitude, the wind is driven by Earth's eastward rotation over the vast open ocean. There is little land that far south to interrupt its power.

(1.5 liters, or 6 cups) each. That meant little enough for drinking, and none for bathing or washing clothes. Laundry could be tied to a rope and dragged in the sea. It was a risky business, though. One convict collecting the washing was swept overboard during stormy weather.

The fleet stopped at Rio de Janeiro, in South America, to pick up new supplies and to give some ill convicts time to recover. The *Lady Penrhyn* was re-stocked with oranges, bananas, and fresh vegetables to prevent scurvy, known by this time to be caused by lack of vitamin C. Two weeks later, the fleet sailed on through rough seas, reaching Cape Town at the southern tip of Africa by mid-November. There the ship picked up horses—the first to be sent to Botany Bay. On the longest leg of the voyage and what could have been the toughest, the First Fleet ships were lucky not to encounter the wild seas tossed by frigid winds in the Roaring Forties (a notorious stretch of the southern ocean). Later fleets did, leaving many ill with scurvy and dysentery, their inadequate clothing making the cold even harder to bear.

After sailing for 252 days, all aboard must have cheered when *Lady Penrhyn* dropped anchor on January 20, 1788, in Botany Bay. There would be no return from this final destination. But at least they'd survived. Or most of them had: 32 convicts had died. Far more people in the Second Fleet—around 278—lost their lives from illness or starvation. Those later convicts were treated cruelly by guards and kept in irons below decks much of the time, beaten for breaking the rules or given little food. Subsequent ships had surgeons in charge of daily routines to ensure the convicts arrived safe and sound.

Australia, at Last

GOVERNOR PHILLIP WAS DISAPPOINTED to discover that Botany Bay was not a good place to build a settlement. Exploring north along the coast, he found that Port Jackson (renamed Sydney, the biggest city in Australia today) had what Botany Bay lacked—ample room in a calmer harbor for all the fleet, plenty of fresh water nearby, and enough space for the settlers. He immediately moved the fleet to Port Jackson and the convicts began the work of clearing land.

A jail or stockade seemed unnecessary. Where could the convicts flee to, except to wilderness? But none were free. Those with carpentry, farming, fishing, or other needed skills began to work off their sentences. They lived in rough wooden huts or tents until they could find enough clay to make sun-dried bricks to build small homes. A criminal court decided punishments for those who broke the rules—flogging or a term on isolated Norfolk Island in a separate small

An 1803 painting of Port Jackson by William John Lancashire, a prisoner sent to Australia for the crime of forgery

CHANGING WEATHER

Scientists have compared weather notes in journals kept by the crew on the First Fleet with modern observations. They've found patterns that suggest the fleet arrived during a wet La Niña year, but that El Niño took over by 1790, causing the drought that led to crop failures and near-starvation for the colony. These Spanish names are given to alternating periods of warm (El Niño) and cool (La Niña) water temperatures in the eastern and western Pacific, which affect the amount of rainfall around the world.

settlement. The fleet had arrived in Australia's midsummer, too late to plant food crops, and the hot, dry climate the next summer meant a meager harvest. In fact, starvation threatened the colony until the arrival of the Second Fleet (6 ships) in 1790, with more provisions. A Third Fleet (11 ships) followed in 1791 to continue what the *Lady Penrhyn* and the other first ships had pioneered.

From then until 1868, single ships came on a regular basis. They established main penal colonies at Van Diemen's Land (now called Tasmania), and in Western Australia convicts reinforced the original population of free settlers from England. In all, about 165,000 convicts were transported to the land down under, a massive undertaking in times when few people other than explorers or merchants made such long sea voyages. Convicts who served out their sentences were granted land for farms, or could choose to set up businesses. They married or were joined by their families from England, and looked ahead to a new life in Australia. For many it was a far better outcome than they could have dreamed of in Newgate Prison.

NOTORIOUS NEWGATE PRISON

For criminals in 18th-century England, Newgate Prison in London must have seemed like the end of the road. Originally built in 1188, rebuilt several times, and used until 1902, it held hundreds awaiting trial or punishment. First offenders and dangerous criminals might share the same crowded cells. Unless prisoners could pay the managers who ran the place for such basics as food, clothing, or a bed, they had to do without. If you died there, as more than half of those awaiting execution did, your corpse remained until your family paid to claim it. There was no proper sanitation, no heat, and little medical attention, since doctors were reluctant to enter because of the terrible smells and fear of disease. Daily executions outside the prison walls attracted spectators; the ghastly sight was intended to discourage crime. While the punishment of Transportation did little to slow the rise in crime, those taken to Australia may have felt fortunate to escape the hangman's noose at Newgate.

An 1872 engraving depicts the exercise yard at Newgate Prison.

In this 1788 painting by Captain Arthur Phillip, the British claim Australia by planting their flag.

Not Such a Good Outcome for All

Iᴛ ᴡᴀꜱ ǫᴜɪᴛᴇ ᴛʜᴇ ᴏᴘᴘᴏꜱɪᴛᴇ for the indigenous people whose country England had occupied. After living by hunting and gathering, mostly isolated from the rest of the world for 50,000 years, they suffered tragic, long-term effects from the arrival of the convict ships. How strange it must have been to see the First Fleet sail into the harbor, unloading hundreds of people who immediately began to cut trees and clear land that wasn't theirs! They would have watched in horror, and anger, as these strangers hunted and fished without asking permission. Governor Phillip traded with the Eora, nomadic people who lived in the immediate area, and tried to teach them the English ways.

Aboriginal leader Bungaree—shown in 1826 wearing a military uniform—encouraged cooperation between his people and white settlers.

But soon thefts of garden tools by the Eora and hunting tools by the convicts led to strained relationships. Within a year, an epidemic of smallpox had ravaged the aboriginal population, who had no resistance to the new disease. Over time, hostilities grew as aboriginal peoples were displaced by expanding settlements. Freed settlers might eventually become prominent citizens in society, but aboriginal people were forced to give up their traditional homelands and treated as slaves. Children were sent to boarding schools and allowed little contact with their families or their culture. Aboriginal people began demanding the right of citizenship in 1938; it wasn't granted until 1967. Today, out of 23 million Australians, less than 700,000 are aboriginal.

invasive species

Seeds and plants from England, along with about 500 animals, also traveled in the First Fleet. The arrival of these new species in Australia began dramatic changes to the balance of nature. Forests of eucalyptus trees were cleared for building and farming, and cattle, sheep, goats, and horses overgrazed and damaged the hard, dry soil. After cats and pigs escaped the settlement, they preyed on indigenous species that had thrived in isolation for thousands of years. Rabbits and blackbirds, both imported from Europe in the late 18th century, have become destructive pests, and the prickly pear cactus has spread to become a harmful weed.

A 1982 Australia Day stamp celebrates the country's varied heritage.

Convict Ancestry

IT'S ESTIMATED THAT ONE IN FIVE Australians can trace their background to a convict settler. Up until the 1970s, this information was largely ignored, even viewed as shameful, and hidden by many. Today, this ancestry—beginning with those aboard ships like the *Lady Penrhyn*—is a source of interest and national pride, a distinctive feature of Australian heritage. People have come to appreciate the resourcefulness and teamwork of those original convicts who built the colonies into an independent nation in a little over 100 years. Each year, on January 26, Australia Day commemorates the birth of the colony at Port Jackson in 1788.

4

USS SUSQUEHANNA

Mission to Japan

NAME
Taken from a river beginning in New York state that flows to Chesapeake Bay on America's east coast. *Susquehanna* and its sister ship, *Mississippi*, were also known as "black ships" for their color.

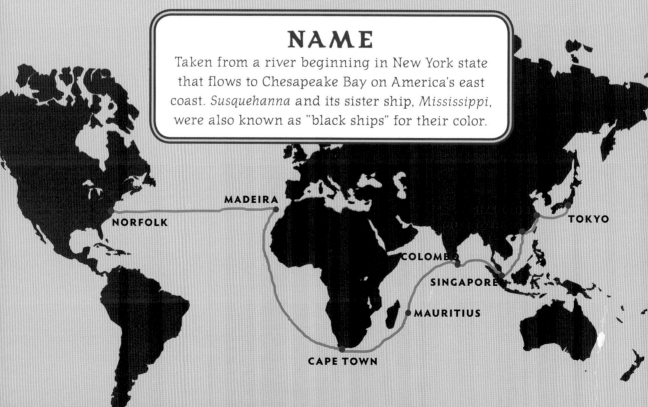

NORFOLK

MADEIRA

CAPE TOWN

COLOMBO

SINGAPORE

MAURITIUS

TOKYO

BUILT

In 1847 at the New York Navy Yard; launched April 5, 1850. It was one of the first ships in the US Navy powered by steam. On June 8, 1851, it became the flagship of the East India Squadron under Matthew C. Perry.

DESCRIPTION

A steam-powered frigate, or warship, with paddle wheels on each side and three masts with square sails. Its top speed was 16.6 kilometers (10 miles) per hour, or 9 knots. It carried 15 large rifles.

CLAIM TO FAME

Sent in 1853 by the United States government to force ruling Japanese shoguns to allow trade with the outside world and to open their coal ports to American steamships. Commodore Perry's successful mission ended Japan's 200-year-old closed-door policy and led to its rapid modernization.

DRAFT: 6 METERS (20 FEET)

WEIGHT: 2,450 TONS

WIDTH: 14 METERS (46 FEET)

LENGTH: 78 METERS (257 FEET)

WHERE IS IT NOW?

The *Susquehanna* left Japanese waters on March 24, 1853, and after operating on the coast of China, returned to America. From 1856 to 1860 it was attached to the Mediterranean Squadron. In the 1860s it took part in the US Civil War, during which it captured British and Confederate schooners, and worked on the Atlantic coast of South America. In 1867 it survived a tsunami after a 7.5-magnitude earthquake in Saint Thomas, in the Caribbean Sea. *Susquehanna* was sold for scrap in 1883 in New York.

JAPAN
[1853]

Kenji drops his heavy bundle, out of breath as he flees with the others from their seaside village. He can't run as fast as his parents and older brothers, and a sense of panic grabs him as he imagines being left behind. Still, he dares to look back.

The choppy waters of Edo Bay teem with dozens of small wooden boats pulled by oarsmen. With the flags of Japan's shogun raised high, they attempt to surround the four strange black warships that belch thick smoke like angry monsters. Kenji knows foreign ships are not allowed to come to this bay, so close to the capital city. Only local fishermen or small craft carrying local goods to markets can sail near the coast, and it is forbidden for anyone to leave Japan. It has been that way for all of Kenji's nine years and, he knows, for generations before.

But these fearsome ships have cannons. Have these outsiders come to make war? Will they try to come ashore? How will they be kept away from the great city of Edo? Carried by the wind across the water, shouts from those in the many guard boats order the intruders to leave.

Kenji also hears his father calling to him to hurry. The news of these foreign ships from America had spread quickly through the small towns and villages. Not knowing what to expect, everyone had been told to move inland, to take what they could carry and to hide from danger. Is that all the people of Japan can do, Kenji worries? His country has no navy to defend its shores from an attack. Will these black ships be the first of many more to come?

With a last look back, Kenji grabs his bundle and runs, his fear giving new power to his legs.

The Story of the USS Susquehanna

IF YOU SAIL INTO TOKYO BAY TODAY, you'll be within Japan's largest industrial area. Over 35 million people live and work close to several of the busiest ports in the whole Asia-Pacific region, all of which welcome ships daily from around the globe. At the head of the bay, modern skyscrapers rise in the capital city. Who would imagine that barely 150 years ago, this bay, and all of Japan, was closed to the outside world? No ships could enter the bay, almost no foreign trade was allowed, and people were forbidden to travel in or out of the country. What happened to bring about such sweeping change? The arrival of one small fleet of American warships, led by USS *Susquehanna*, was the first step in breaking down Japan's 200-year-old barriers.

Shogun Power

DURING JAPAN'S EARLY HISTORY, medieval landowners rose to wealth and power in the largely agricultural economy. They developed into a class called *samurai*, or warriors. By the 13th century, they held authority over lower classes—farmers, artisans, and merchants—and frequently fought with each other. By the 1600s, samurai leaders, called *shoguns*, ruled the country in place of the emperor, whose role had become mainly ceremonial. Meanwhile, Japan had become part of a trading network with Europeans who were doing business in Indonesia and China. As the shoguns' power grew, so did their concern that foreign nations might try to take over Japan. Already, Portuguese Jesuit missionaries had managed to convert thousands of Japanese Buddhists to Christianity. The shoguns decided a change in foreign policy was needed. Japan must turn its back on the rest of the world. Christians were expelled in 1638. Severe limitations were put on shipbuilding to keep the Japanese people at home, and foreign ships that entered Japanese waters were attacked or destroyed. Japan's outside contact shrank to a small amount of trade under tight restrictions, and only through the port of Nagasaki. For 200 years, Japan remained closed, relying almost totally on its own resources. But inside this safe zone, the economy thrived, roads were built, and cities grew into vibrant commercial and cultural centers.

An 1867 illustration of fighting samurai

Trading by Steamship

THIS WAS STILL THE SITUATION in the mid-1800s, when American politicians sought ways to spread their culture, trade, and religion overseas. They found several reasons to want to establish contact with Japan. The most pressing one had to do with the Pacific shipping trade. At the time, the United States had the fastest clipper ships, which carried trade goods—tea, silk, and spices—home from Europe and Asia. But countries using steamships, like Britain, were gaining the advantage in the Atlantic shipping trade. More efficient and dependable than clippers, steamships didn't have to rely on favorable winds. They did need coal, and to reach Japan across the Pacific from the United States (almost one and a half times the distance across the Atlantic to Europe) would take more coal than a ship could carry in those days. There might be another way, though—using coal supplies from ports along the west coast and north past Alaska. Once the US government learned that Japan had significant amounts of coal, the merchants had the final piece of the fuel supply puzzle.

CLIPPER SHIPS

Clippers—fast, tall sailing ships—were developed in America in the mid-1800s especially to carry cargos of tea from China to the Tea Exchange in London, England. With huge sails aloft, they often raced each other, as the first to bring the new season's crop of tea fetched the highest prices at auction. The fastest clippers, like the famous *Cutty Sark*, might overtake a steamship on the high seas. But once the Suez Canal in Egypt opened in 1869, steam-powered vessels could sail between the Mediterranean Sea and the Indian Ocean in far less time than it took a clipper ship to round the southern tip of Africa.

A Dutch painting from around 1700 depicts whaling ships.

America needed to grab a share of the trade in the Far East, and quickly. US politicians had seen how Britain had gained entry into China by means of a treaty signed after the Opium Wars of 1840. Meanwhile, ships from Russia, Holland, and France had begun to compete for trade. In the race to establish a foothold, America was determined to win the first entry into Japan. Then the way would also be clear to establish further trade, and Christian missions, in China and beyond.

Another issue spurred the Americans to try to break down Japan's barriers. For years, American whalers had fished close to Japan. Whale oil was in high demand as fuel for lamps, and it kept factory machines running smoothly. But if the ships got into trouble in storms, they had no safe refuge. The Japanese saw them as Christian intruders, so their ships were often fired upon and the sailors captured or executed. It was time to demand that the Japanese government offer safety and fair treatment to shipwrecked sailors.

A SEAGOING PADDLE-WHEEL STEAMSHIP

Within the black hull of the *Susquehanna*, all that was required for a six-month sea voyage was crammed into four decks. In the lowest deck—the hold—water tanks, coal storage, and ammunition took up considerable space. A boiler, the funnel, and two massive paddle wheels—each 9.4 meters (31 feet) in diameter and as high as a three-story building—occupied the entire mid-ship section. One deck above—called the lower tween deck—storage compartments held sails, equipment, and food. The officers' cabins and crew quarters with hammocks shared the upper tween deck with a medical room. The main deck housed cannons and guns and the wheelhouse. The goats and poultry on board provided fresh food. Three masts with square-rigged sails rose above the main deck.

The Voyage Begins

Wɪᴛʜ ᴛʜᴇsᴇ ɢᴏᴀʟs ɪɴ ᴍɪɴᴅ, an expedition of four warships set sail from Norfolk, Virginia, in 1852. An American naval officer, Matthew Perry, led the fleet on the steamship *Susquehanna* across the Atlantic, around the southern tip of Africa to the Indian Ocean, following the trading route to the East opened 350 years earlier by Vasco da Gama. Six months later, by the spring of 1853, Japan's main islands were sighted.

When the black-hulled, paddle-wheeled *Susquehanna* entered the Uraga Channel leading to Tokyo Bay on July 8, 1853, the Japanese were horrified. Barbarians, so close to Japan's capital city! These black ships belching steam were far more intimidating than anything the Japanese had seen before. Dozens of small boats flying the shoguns' flag surrounded Commodore Perry's ships, ordering them to leave immediately.

Clever Tactics

Iɴᴛɪᴍɪᴅᴀᴛɪᴏɴ, ʙᴜᴛ ᴡɪᴛʜᴏᴜᴛ ᴠɪᴏʟᴇɴᴄᴇ, was exactly what Perry wanted. His mission was to present a strong showing of power to impress the Japanese with America's supremacy. *Susquehanna* bristled with guns, ready to repel any attempts to board the vessels. Perry ignored repeated orders from the Japanese officials to depart and did not appear on deck, insisting that he would only speak to a direct representative of the emperor. Perry had done his homework, studying the Japanese culture and learning all he could turn to his advantage to deal with people he knew would not welcome him. By remaining aloof and firm, Perry believed he would gain

their respect—and he had carefully chosen gifts ready to amaze. These included valuable editions of natural history books by John James Audubon, champagne, perfume, a telegraph machine, a camera, finely crafted Colt weapons, and a small-scale model of a steam-powered railway train. As if the *Susquehanna* itself was not remarkable enough, these gifts would show the Japanese how prosperous and highly developed America had become.

A standoff followed. The Japanese insisted Perry take his ships back to dock at Nagasaki. Perry refused to back down. In fact, he sent survey ships farther up the bay, ever closer to the largely unprotected city of Edo. Tension mounted. Over several days, the two sides almost came to blows. Eventually, with the threat of superior firepower, Perry's ships prevailed.

When Japanese officials finally agreed to the high-level meeting, they hoped to buy time rather than give in to the aggressors. Perry went ashore on July 14, making sure he was backed up by 250 armed soldiers and gunboats in case of trickery. He presented his papers, including a letter to the Japanese emperor from American president Millard Fillmore. It was wrapped in a special, artistically decorated box—Perry knew the Japanese liked formality. The letter requested the right to buy coal, protection for shipwrecked American seamen, and the opening of more ports to trade.

Time to Compromise

AFTER THE MEETING, Perry told his hosts he would return within a year to hear the emperor's response to his requests. He hung around a few more days doing surveys of possible future anchorages in the bay—to show he was still in control—before sailing to Hong Kong, where he planned to spend the winter. But after hearing that French and Russian ships might be approaching Japan with their own trading treaties, he decided to return in February. This time, *Susquehanna* led a fleet of nine ships with 1,800 men.

The Japanese were by no means happy to give in to the American demands yet. The group most opposed to change, the shoguns, felt the country should resist all encounters with foreigners. They saw how China's ruling dynasty had declined after the British and French gained entry. Another group more willing to negotiate felt Japan might be better off giving in a little to avoid a total takeover.

A painting from 1855 depicts Perry and his crew on their return to Japan.

Because they had been learning about world events from the few traders they dealt with—for instance, they knew how the Industrial Revolution had brought about advances in technology all across Europe—they realized Japan was falling behind. As well, Japan's economy was suffering because of the high taxes needed to support the large samurai class. Still unsure, the Japanese tried to stall Perry again with offers of limited trade. Again Perry stood firm. Without a navy, Japanese officials knew they could not keep out any intruders for long.

On March 31, 1854, the Kanagawa Treaty was signed, giving America trading access to the ports of Shimoda (near Tokyo) and Hakodate (on the north island of Hokkaido). Further negotiations soon opened other ports. The Japanese agreed to sell coal to American steamships and to offer help to shipwrecked sailors. In short, Perry was able to gain all of his requests that day—with the exception of a wish to enter the magnificent capital city, Edo. To this, the Japanese could not agree. Perry had to settle for viewing it from the deck of the *Susquehanna*.

A New Era for Japan

EVEN THOUGH MANY JAPANESE still opposed change after Perry's visit, Western influences quickly flowed into Japan. Trade brought foreign goods, cultural ideas, and money into the country, which upset the economic order. The people became dissatisfied with shogun rule and their power ended by 1868. The forces of the emperor took over, beginning what is known as the Meiji Restoration. More treaties were signed, with Britain, Russia, and Holland. The country had a lot of catching up to do. Once the people saw what other countries were doing in science and education, and how their military powers were developing, students were sent to America and Europe to learn more.

In turn, these travelers spread aspects of Japanese culture—its art, literature, and music—to the rest of the world. Japan began its own version of Europe's Industrial Revolution.

Modernization of the military became a key goal for Japan. Japanese leaders wanted to make their military strong enough to prevent any takeover by another nation. The result? Within 50 years of the *Susquehanna*'s arrival in Tokyo Bay, Japan was on its way to becoming one of the world's great naval powers. It exercised that might up until its Second World War battles in the Pacific against America—the very country that had started Japan on its remarkable progress toward becoming a modern nation.

BLACK SHIPS REMEMBERED

In 1945, Tokyo Bay was the site of the Japanese surrender to the Allies after the Second World War. Almost 100 years after Perry's black ships had opened up Japan, a flag preserved from one of his ships flew high during the surrender ceremonies.

5

H.L. HUNLEY

An Undersea Weapon

NAME

From its wealthy benefactor and designer,
Horace L. Hunley

SOUTH CAROLINA
USA

• H.L. HUNLEY

BUILT

Designed by James McClintock, H.L. Hunley, and Lieutenant George Dixon. Constructed at Tredegar Iron Works, Richmond, Virginia, in 1863, and launched at Mobile, Alabama.

DESCRIPTION

A streamlined log-shaped submarine with two conning towers (small raised compartments with the instruments and controls), diving planes (flat surfaces, much like rudders) that could be used to guide the sub up and down, and a depth gauge. It was operated by means of a hand-cranked propeller. Its spar—a 5-meter (16-foot) iron pole attached to the bow—had a copper tip carrying black powder explosive.

CLAIM TO FAME

The *Hunley* played a small role in the US Civil War, but a large role in the development of undersea warfare and exploration. One of the earliest submarines, it was the first to sink a warship and paved the way for further submarine technology.

WIDTH:
1 METER
(3 FEET)

HEIGHT:
1.3 METERS
(4 FEET)

LENGTH: 13 METERS (42 FEET)

WHERE IS IT NOW?

Although it sank in 1864, the *Hunley* was not found until May 7, 1995, off the South Carolina coast. Raised in 2000, it's now under study by archaeologists at the Warren Lasch Conservation Center in North Charleston, South Carolina.

On Board RMS Lusitania [May 7, 1915]

Avis manages to finish her lunch of chicken and vegetables—one of the few meals she's been able to face after being seasick practically the whole way across the Atlantic from New York. The conversation among others at the table does little to calm her jittery stomach, though. Some say the Lusitania is taking a serious risk since Germany has declared this area a war zone. Avis has already heard the stories of German U-boats—submarines being used as weapons—lurking in the deep, dark channel between England and Ireland. But after her first glimpse of the coast of Ireland when the fog lifted this morning, she feels safe enough.

Suddenly a powerful explosion rocks the ship. Then, another. Avis grabs the table as the world tilts. Food and dishes clatter to the floor. On the sharply listing deck, chaos erupts. The rush to get life belts on, the screams and jostling of the passengers trying to climb into lifeboats...it's a blur of confusion and noise and terror.

A man urges Avis to scramble across a deck chair bridging the gap to a small boat hanging out over the waves. She can't believe how fast this huge ship is sinking; only minutes have passed but it is already half underwater on this side. She shudders as the crew begins to lower the lifeboat. Two men leap from the railing and Avis feels the jolt as one of them lands awkwardly. The boat rolls onto its side, spilling everyone out.

Avis has no time even to scream before the freezing water closes over her head. Her lungs are about to burst as she struggles to the surface, trying to swim. Someone seizes her arm and drags her onto a raft. Gasping and coughing up seawater, Avis gives in to a rush of hot tears. All around, people struggle in the water, calling for help. How did this innocent voyage to school in England turn to disaster?

The Story of H.L. Hunley

THREE SCIENTISTS PEERED from the viewport of the minisubmarine at the massive ocean liner resting in its North Atlantic grave. Photographs taken that day in 1986 of the ghostly remains of the *Titanic* lying 3,784 meters (12,415 feet) beneath the surface would stun the world. It's hard to imagine that the inspiration for that 20th-century minisubmarine was a simple vessel developed 120 years earlier as a weapon of war. How did it contribute to today's exciting undersea investigation possibilities? Once inventors overcame puzzling technological challenges, they went on to develop a new class of ship—the submarine—that would change the course of history. This ship would allow people to function in an alien environment filled with danger—much like outer space.

An Impossible Dream?

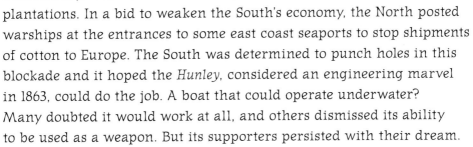

A CIGAR-SHAPED CRAFT about as long as a school bus but only half as wide, *H.L. Hunley* was the great-grandfather of modern submersibles. The *Hunley* was built to defy a Union blockade of Confederate shipping during the US Civil War (1861–65). In this deadly conflict, the North (the Union) opposed the South (the Confederacy) over the use of slavery on Southern cotton plantations. In a bid to weaken the South's economy, the North posted warships at the entrances to some east coast seaports to stop shipments of cotton to Europe. The South was determined to punch holes in this blockade and it hoped the *Hunley*, considered an engineering marvel in 1863, could do the job. A boat that could operate underwater? Many doubted it would work at all, and others dismissed its ability to be used as a weapon. But its supporters persisted with their dream.

Built of iron in a streamlined shape much like today's submarines, the *Hunley* had no engine. Instead, seven crew members sat on a bench to crank a propeller by hand. Hand power also worked pumps to fill and empty ballast tanks with water, which was how the ship was lowered and raised. It could only stay submerged for a couple of hours. It's hard to believe such a ship—so primitive by today's standards—managed to sink an enemy warship five times its size.

An 1861 illustration of ships blockading Charleston Harbor

The Voyage Begins

THE SUBMARINE'S MAIN OBJECTIVE was to torpedo and sink the Union warships patrolling the sea outside Charleston, South Carolina. But in its first training run in the harbor with a crew of eight army personnel, it sank after being swamped and unbalanced by a passing ship. Three men had to fight their way out, but five others were trapped, and died. The catastrophic sinking, and recovery of the submarine from 12 meters (40 feet) of water, had to be kept secret if it was going to remain a surprise weapon. Financial supporter Horace Hunley still had faith in his ship. For the next test run, he brought in a more experienced crew to join him. What could possibly go wrong? In fact, Hunley himself is believed to have made a fatal mistake in regulating the amount of water in one of the ballast tanks, flooding the ship. It hit bottom, nose first. This time, all of the crew drowned, including Hunley.

HORACE L. HUNLEY

If you believe strongly in a cause, you might be prepared to contribute time and money to see it succeed. Horace L. Hunley, a wealthy businessman, went even further than that to support the South's bid for independence over the issue of slavery. He understood how crucial it was to keep seaports open both for sales of cotton and for imports of the many goods needed to fight the war against the North—including basic things like boots and machinery, which the agricultural South could not produce. That's why he helped design and pay for the submarine he believed could sink the Northern warships blocking the ports.

Though technology has advanced, the streamlined shape of submarines has stayed much the same since the *Hunley*.

When many were ready to give up on the ill-fated submarine, its new commander was not. Lieutenant George Dixon felt the vessel could do the job it was meant to do. On the night of February 17, 1864, the *Hunley* cruised slowly through the murky harbor water. Bright moonlight meant a high risk of being seen, but the date was likely chosen because of the timing of the tides: ebb tide would help carry the *Hunley* out of the harbor, and the rising tide would give the crew a boost to get it back. It was exhausting work cranking that propeller! The target was the USS *Housatonic*, a Union warship positioned a short distance outside the harbor.

A Not-So-Successful Attack

As the submarine drew near, some of *Housatonic*'s crew mistook it for a log just below the surface. But the steady nature of its progress finally set off alarms. It was too late, though. The *Hunley*'s torpedo, fastened to the end of a rod the length of an Olympic pole vaulter's, made contact with the warship. At least 41 kilograms (90 pounds) of black powder explosive blew a huge hole in the *Housatonic*, and it sank within five minutes.

After delivering its fatal blow, the *Hunley* disappeared...for a third time. It was lost, along with the entire crew, and mystery would shadow the event for over 130 years. Was this a victory for the *Hunley*? Its attack may only have raised temporary fears in the North that the Confederates had more of these dastardly weapons. Yet while it paid dearly for its single successful attack, this pioneer submersible proved that undersea warfare was possible. Despite the fact that Charleston surrendered to the North only a year later, the stage was set for far bigger things for submarines.

The *Hunley* is brought to the surface in 2000, 136 years after its sinking.

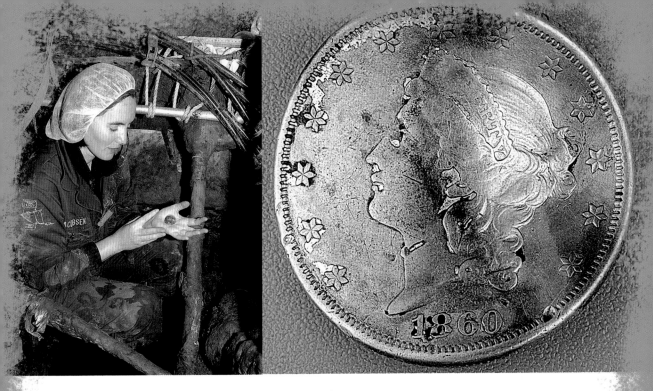

Archaeologist Maria Jacobsen
with a coin found in the *Hunley*

HUNLEY GIVES UP ITS SECRETS

H.L. Hunley was astonishingly well preserved after 131 years in salt water. Archaeologists studying the recovered submarine have found bones, teeth, hair, and scraps of brain tissue, from which they've obtained DNA that has helped identify some of the crew. Other discoveries include a 20-dollar gold coin and even fingerprints, imprinted into the crusty shell of concrete-hard mud and sediment inside the ship.

To preserve the outer hull, that shell was left in place until 2014. Then, to dissolve it, the ship was soaked for months in a chemical solution. Next, archaeologists began to carefully remove the crust using dental tools. Once it's removed, they'll see how the *Hunley* really looked, and maybe solve the biggest mystery: why it sank. The cleaned hull could reveal holes—perhaps where it was pierced by bullets fired from the *Housatonic*—or damage to the ship caused by the shock of its own exploding torpedo.

Submarine Progress

TECHNOLOGY ADVANCED SLOWLY through the 1800s. The development of the periscope permitted stealthy observation while a ship was still submerged. After all, such a ship would only be effective in wartime if it remained mostly invisible to the enemy. It took several decades to find a satisfactory power source, though. Obviously the *Hunley*'s hand-cranking system was doomed to failure. The most promising development, in 1898, was American inventor John P. Holland's diesel-fueled engine. While operating on the surface, the engine charged electric batteries for quiet underwater cruising. Holland's system became the standard way to propel submarines until the mid-1900s, when nuclear-powered submarines were created. Today, instead of only being able to work barely below the surface for a couple of hours, subs can journey around the globe at depths of over 460 meters (1,500 feet)—that's the height of Toronto's CN Tower.

One more feature—the torpedo—would undergo drastic upgrading from the spar-mounted weapon used by the *Hunley*. The serious limitations of having to get so close to a ship to deliver the destructive blow—like having to sneak right up to the enemy with a knife—were overcome by the invention, in England in 1866, of a self-propelled torpedo. That was more like firing a bullet at a target from a good distance away. Once sent on its

UP PeRISCOPe!

The periscope, a device using mirrors and prisms in a tube to permit observation from a hidden position— for instance, underwater—was invented in 1902.

The remains of the *Hunley*, now under study in South Carolina

way from a tube in the submarine, a torpedo is pushed through the water by a small engine using a battery or special fuel. Its explosive tip detonates on contact with an object, ideally an enemy ship's hull. And the submarine that fires the device can be a safe distance away— something that might have saved the *Hunley*.

CRUISING UNDER ARCTIC ICE

The first nuclear-powered US Navy submarine, *Nautilus*, took a crew of 116 under thick Arctic ice to the North Pole on August 3, 1958. This achievement marked the first time any ship had reached the North Pole—even the toughest icebreakers at the time couldn't get there. In addition to proving the extraordinary capabilities of nuclear-powered subs, the journey resulted in new discoveries about the Arctic Ocean.

A Weapon of War,
a Tool in Peacetime

THE SUBMARINE, now ready for combat, was a fearsome
weapon during the First and Second World Wars. Germany built
the U-boat—"undersea boat"—fitted with torpedoes and deck guns,
and began to sink commercial ships in 1914. It stunned the world by
targeting the British ocean liner *Lusitania* a year later. Germany's
attacks took such a heavy toll that it came close to gaining command
of the seas and winning the war. In the Second World War, Germany's
U-boats stopped supplies of everything from food to ammunition from
reaching the British Isles from North America. Engineers put their
skills to the test coming up with weapons to defend against U-boats
in the Battle of the Atlantic. And in the Pacific, US submarines sank
more than one third of Japan's Navy, along with 5 million tons of its
commercial shipping, trying to force it to surrender. Then, in the

1950s, growing tensions between the US and USSR led both countries to build up their arsenal of submarines.

Today's modern submersible vessels are used in peacetime, too. For instance, nuclear submarines are now used to conduct studies to measure the thickness of polar ice and to map the ocean floor under ice caps.

They may also assist in scientific exploration and archaeology, underwater photography, servicing undersea equipment, and for rescue missions if someone is trapped in a sunken vessel. Some of these craft can venture to incredible depths, where they withstand crushing pressure. Given the ever-present dangers of working underwater, safety equipment and escape systems have been invented to deal with emergencies. Today, the tragic loss of life experienced by the crew of *H.L. Hunley* is far less likely to happen.

ANTI-SUBMARINE DEFENSES

The ability of submarines to travel unseen by ships on the surface has made them lethal instruments of war. To counter this threat during the First World War, an anti-submarine weapon called a depth charge was developed. Thrown from a destroyer, this bomb in a steel drum exploded at a preset depth where submarines lurked. Britain came up with Q-ships, which bore weaponry disguised as deckhouses and lifeboats, fooling submarines into surfacing close enough to be fired upon. By 1917, convoys—large groups of merchant ships escorted by heavily armed destroyers—helped more supplies safely reach Britain from North America. Anti-submarine nets installed across the opening of a harbor could prevent submarines from sneaking close to major ports, such as Halifax, Nova Scotia. Nets were even strung across parts of the English Channel to keep enemy subs away from Britain's shores.

The outbreak of the Second World War saw a more sophisticated type of submarine in action, and new technologies had to be found to fight them. One was sonar, a system that can detect engine noise from a submarine, or bounce sound waves off a submerged object to locate it.

SINKING OF *KURSK*

Even with advanced submarine technology, dangers still exist. In 2000, the crew of the Russian nuclear submarine *Kursk* met a similar fate to that of the *Hunley* over 130 years earlier. *Kursk* was taking part in exercises in the Barents Sea, north of Russia, when a torpedo failed due to leaking fuel. Two massive explosions rocked the ship. It sank in 108 meters (354 feet) of water—think of a 35-story building—leaving only 23 of 118 crew members still alive in one compartment near the stern. Attempts to rescue them with a small submersible proved impossible as the submarine was lying at an angle that prevented entry. It was two months before divers were able to enter the ship. Sadly, they discovered the 23 trapped crew had survived only several hours, long enough to write notes to help explain the tragedy. The *Kursk* was salvaged in May 2001.

High-Tech Subs

AND WHAT ABOUT THOSE MINISUBMARINES used by scientists? Their "weapons" are cameras and recording equipment, and they can only operate within a small area. They are lifted out of the water after examining sea life or sunken objects and transported back to land aboard a support ship. In 1986, the minisub *Alvin* took scientists into the depths for that first look at the *Titanic* since its sinking in 1912. In 2014, unmanned robotic submersibles were used in the search for the missing Malaysia Airlines Flight 370, believed to have crashed into the southern Indian Ocean off Australia.

Imagine traveling around the globe underwater in a long, narrow ship with everything you and more than 100 other people will need. Your workplace may have limited space, with no windows, but it has most of the comforts of home, thanks to modern technology. Today's submariners work in this demanding environment, cruising under the sea, training, patrolling, and gathering intelligence and

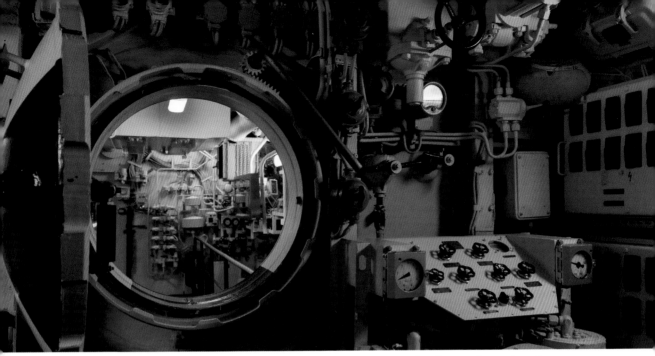

Inside a modern submarine

scientific data. Submarines are considered elite craft that use highly sophisticated equipment to protect friendly shipping, and weapons to defend against hostilities. What was considered cutting-edge technology in 1863 when the *Hunley* made its ill-fated trip has evolved to turn the dream of sailing under the sea into reality.

MAKING HISTORY FROM HISTORY

In 1845, British explorer Sir John Franklin set out to find the Northwest Passage through the Canadian Arctic. His two ships, HMS *Erebus* and HMS *Terror*, were lost after becoming icebound, and 129 men perished. In 2014, submersible sonar imaging equipment towed behind a research ship found *Erebus* at the bottom of Queen Maud Gulf. Both expeditions— the ships from history and today's submarine-inspired technology—had the same goal: to further understanding of the world's oceans.

6

KOMAGATA MARU
Unwelcome Passengers

NAME

Previously used by a German company to ferry immigrants from Europe to North America under the names SS *Stubbenhuk* and SS *Sicilia*, it was sold in 1913 to a Japanese company and renamed *Komagata Maru* (*maru* means "circle" and is often used in Japanese ship names).

VICTORIA

YOKOHAMA

KOBE

MOJI

HONG KONG

BUILT

In 1890, launched by Charles Connell and Co. of Scotland

DESCRIPTION

A cargo steamship, its lower deck was cleaned and fitted with latrines and 533 wooden benches.

CLAIM TO FAME

In 1914, the *Komagata Maru* sailed from Hong Kong to Vancouver, British Columbia, carrying 376 passengers from India. When they were not allowed to land in Canada, it sparked an international incident, revealing injustices and eventually leading to big changes in immigration rules.

**WIDTH:
12 METERS
(41 FEET)**

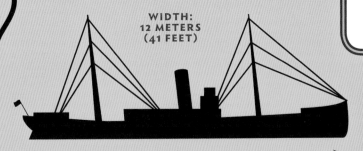

LENGTH: 100 METERS (329 FEET)

WHERE IS IT NOW?

The ship, renamed *Heian Maru* in 1924, was wrecked at Cape Soyedomari, Hokkaido, Japan, on February 11, 1926.

VANCOUVER
[July 1914]

It's early when Indar relieves the guard posted at the stern of the Komagata Maru. His stomach growls with the hunger that kept him awake most of the night. But there is no food and only a little water left from the supplies delivered to the ship several weeks ago. Nevertheless, Indar must take his turn on the watch, posted after the violent confrontation with police and immigration officers two days earlier. No one is certain what will happen next.

He can still remember the crowd's angry roar and see the missiles of coal and bricks hurled at those on the tugboat trying to board the Komagata Maru. After a fellow Sikh took an axe to the line the police had tied to their ship, the tug had finally backed off. The passengers won that skirmish, but it has left everyone aboard wary and on edge.

Now Indar gazes out at the golden sunrise spreading across Vancouver's harbor. The crowds that gather on the docks are gone, for now. They come every morning, many with signs he cannot read but that others say are ordering the immigrants to go home. Has his family back in India heard what has happened here? He has only 10 dollars in his pocket, far short of the 200 dollars he needs to enter Canada. But as a citizen of the British Empire, he thinks it is worth taking the chance. He brings no threat—only the wish for a job that will pay enough that he can send money home to help his family keep their farm.

He thinks again of his dream to return to that farm one day. He faces westward, toward India . . . and his heart leaps to his throat. A warship is steaming toward the Komagata Maru. He shouts to raise the alarm. Will he ever see his home again?

The Story of the Komagata Maru

Pᴇᴏᴘʟᴇ ᴍᴏᴠᴇ ʙᴇᴛᴡᴇᴇɴ ᴄᴏᴜɴᴛʀɪᴇꜱ for many reasons. Sometimes they immigrate to a new country for a good job, or to be with other family members already living there. They may be looking for freedom from restrictive government or religious rules. Anyone who wishes to live in a new country is usually welcome if they meet its immigration requirements. But in the early 20th century, being accepted into Canada depended mostly on where you came from, and people from some countries weren't welcome at all. For a time, one country on this list of exclusions was India.

On May 21, 1914, a steamship called the *Komagata Maru* dropped anchor not far offshore from the city of Vancouver, British Columbia. On board were 376 South Asians, many of whom were farmers, who had traveled from India, seeking jobs and a better life in Canada. Even though the countries they traveled between were both part of the British Empire, they were met with a wall of opposition: laws had been passed by the Canadian government to keep them from entering the country. At the same time, Canada was encouraging immigration from European countries by offering free passage and farmland. What was the reason for this unwelcome reception for nonwhite British subjects?

India Struggles for Equality

FROM THE EARLY 17TH CENTURY, India had been largely controlled by the British East India Company, which had established trading posts there. In the mid-19th century, the British government took over management of the country. Queen Victoria was proclaimed Empress of India in 1877, and the land was then known as British India until 1947, when India obtained independence. However, in the early 1900s, Indians became unhappy with British rule, feeling they were overtaxed and not given fair chances at jobs or government positions that would help them improve their standard of living. They formed organizations to try to bring about equality between Indian and British citizens. Some of those organizations started groups in other countries, like Canada, encouraging Indians living overseas to voice their support for the struggle. Britain resisted changes, concerned about losing the tax income it gained from India. Discontented Indian citizens began to look outside their country for better opportunities.

A New Life in a New Land?

SINCE CITIZENS OF INDIA were British subjects, they believed they could move to any other part of the British Empire, including Canada. After all, in the 1800s, many South Asians had gone to British colonies in the Caribbean as workers, and had been allowed to stay and live there after working for five years. Others had served in the British Indian Army, helping Britain expand its control over parts of India, and supported Britain's conflicts in China, the Middle East, and Africa. The soldiers had even traveled to Queen Victoria's Diamond Jubilee celebrations in London in 1887, and King Edward VII's coronation in 1902. Many had found work in other British-owned colonies, so why not immigrate to Canada?

Obstacles to this plan would prove impossible to overcome. In Canada, the mainly European population feared and resented the arrival of too many nonwhite immigrants. To limit their numbers, the Liberal government created the Immigration Act in 1910, which stated that unskilled workers would not be welcome as they would take lower-paying jobs away from Canadians at a time of already high

Indian troops serving Britain in the First World War

unemployment. The description "unskilled worker" fit most of the would-be immigrants from South Asia, as well as those from countries such as China and Japan.

But the regulation that seemed to be directed at India in particular was the Continuous Passage Act, passed two years earlier. It stated that a migrant from Asia must complete the journey from his country of birth to Canada without stopping in other countries along the way. To add another difficulty, Canadian shipping companies were told not to sell passenger tickets in India. So even if South Asians could have bought a ticket, every ship stopped in China, Japan, or Hawaii on the long trip to Canadian ports. How could they possibly meet the Continuous Passage regulation? On top of that, each passenger was required to have the equivalent of 200 US dollars—a large amount for most migrants, whose main reason for traveling to Canada was to find paying work. While about 2,000 Indians, mostly Sikhs—a major religious group with origins in India's northern Punjab region—already lived in Canada, the government clearly wanted to limit further immigration. Canadian officials also worried that new Indian immigrants would join known activists working to stir up hostilities against Britain.

NOT WANTED!

South Asians were not the only immigrants Canada did not make welcome. Even though up to 15,000 Chinese workers had been recruited for low pay to build the Canadian Pacific Railroad in the late 1800s, they were discouraged from staying in Canada once that job was finished. And new Chinese immigrants were charged an entry fee of $50 each—called a "head tax" (it was raised to $500 in 1903). People of Japanese ancestry faced the same racial discrimination after Japan attacked the US Navy in Pearl Harbor, Hawaii, in 1941. Because of the fear they might aid an invasion on the west coast of North America, all Japanese families—even those who had been born in North America—were rounded up and their property was taken away. They were imprisoned in camps away from the coast until after the war.

Japanese Americans and Canadians were held at "relocation centers" like this one in California.

Challenging the Law

A SUCCESSFUL SIKH BUSINESSMAN, Gurdit Singh believed in equal rights for all Indian citizens, and wanted to help make India stronger as it moved toward independence. One nonviolent way was to allow people to emigrate and find work for far better wages in Canada. They could send back money to help their families keep their homes and farms going. In 1914 Singh rented a cargo ship in Hong Kong—the *Komagata Maru*—paid to refit it with wooden benches in the hold to carry passengers, and sold one-way tickets to Vancouver. He loaded a shipment of coal that he planned to sell to help pay for the venture.

Timing was key for Singh's project. He believed his passengers could be allowed to enter Canada because of an incident in Vancouver a year earlier. A group of Sikhs had arrived by boat and, as expected, had been held in custody until officials could apply the law that would turn them away. But the group's lawyer had immediately challenged the Continuous Passage Act in court, and won on the grounds that it was unlawful due to the way it was written in Canada's constitution. Singh hoped the *Komagata Maru* would reach Vancouver before changes to this regulation were made.

Passengers on the
Komagata Maru

The Voyage Begins

AFTER STOPOVERS IN Hong Kong, China, and Japan, the voyage to Vancouver was uneventful. Upon arrival, the ship stopped at Victoria for the required health inspection, and no contagious diseases were found among the passengers. But in Vancouver's harbor, it was prevented from docking and ordered to anchor offshore. British Columbian officials knew if the migrants landed, they could demand a court hearing to argue—and possibly win—against the Continuous Passage regulation. If they were kept on the ship instead, they technically would not be taken into custody. That was important because, once arrested, a British subject had the right to a speedy court hearing.

The immigration inspector found other ways to delay dealing with the migrants, often ignoring the law to do so. Their lawyer was not allowed on board the ship, making communication difficult. The passengers were given little food, water, or medical attention. When the inspector learned that a payment of $15,000 was due to the ship rental company in Hong Kong, Gurdit Singh was prevented from unloading and selling his cargo of coal to raise the money. Without that payment, the company could demand that the ship return to Hong Kong. If that happened, Canada would be spared the dilemma of whether to turn the ship away.

Habeas Corpus

Habeas corpus is the name given to a court order that originated in British law. It states that one's freedom cannot be denied for long without being allowed a legal court hearing.

Tangled in Regulations

Delays dragged on for weeks. The authorities in Vancouver were anxious to prevent people they saw as unsuitable from coming to Canada. If the migrants won in court, Canada would have to accept them or appear to be openly prejudiced against South Asians. Such obvious unfairness would stir up even more anger in the already agitated Vancouver South Asian community. And in India it would only encourage the more militant members of the independence movement, something Britain didn't want. Tensions grew in this political tug-of-war, with its uncertain outcome.

A committee of Sikhs in Vancouver raised money to pay off the rent due on the ship. Twenty-two of the *Komagata Maru*'s passengers were allowed to land in late June because they had lived in Canada once before. Medical examinations for the rest were drawn out over many days. Finally, the shore committee and the immigration officials reached an agreement to take one migrant to court, as a test case. The same judgment would then apply to all the others waiting on the ship.

Even though the lawyer argued that Canada could not legally reject someone on the basis of his race, the court ordered the man deported back to India.

It seemed the immigrants' battle was lost, but they refused to back down easily. The passengers demanded food for the return journey and took over the ship to prevent the captain from sailing. A tugboat sent to intervene was pelted with chunks of coal and driven off. A Royal Canadian Navy ship came to keep order, and troops were put on standby in case of riots on shore. But the use of force was the last thing anyone wanted. The standoff continued until, eventually, the *Komagata Maru* was given provisions and on July 23, two months after arriving in the harbor, it sailed away. When it arrived back in India, authorities there saw the passengers as troublemakers and ordered them to return to their homes in the Punjab region. Most refused to go and 21 died in a confrontation. Violence followed in Vancouver, too, between authorities and the Sikhs who had tried to help the migrants. And as predicted, tensions were inflamed in India, where the struggle for independence continued until the country eventually separated from Britain in 1947.

Canadian officials on board the *Komagata Maru*

"BOaT PeOPLe"

Nearly 800,000 refugees fled Vietnam by boat between 1975 and 1995, including this group awaiting rescue in 1984.

Desperate people fleeing violence or unreasonable restrictions often try to reach safety and freedom by boat. They may pay a huge price, often imposed by people taking advantage of them to make money, for a long and dangerous passage. But they may see it as the best way for many to travel together, and to avoid the checks by authorities they'd face if they tried to board an airplane. If not stopped at sea—or worse, as often the vessels are rundown and liable to sink—the first legal challenges might come as they step ashore at their destination, hoping they will be allowed to stay.

Slow but Steady Change

WHAT HAD BEEN ACHIEVED? Were Canada's immigration laws written in stone? Or would this incident make it easier for South Asians to move to Canada? Not immediately, but gradual changes did come. After the First World War, South Asians already in Canada were allowed to bring their families from India. In 1947, they were given back the right to vote (which had been taken away in 1907). That same year, the Continuous Passage Act was canceled and replaced with new immigration laws. Three years later, 150 people per year were allowed to come from India to Canada. By 1957, that number had doubled. All references to race were removed from Canada's immigration laws in 1967, opening doors to people from many countries.

It was not until 2008 that the province of British Columbia formally apologized for the *Komagata Maru* incident. Canada's Prime Minister has also apologized to the South Asian community. Today, South Asians and others observe their rich cultural heritage in Canada, a right won, in part, after an immigrant ship challenged intolerance and brought it to the world's attention.

A colorful pattern called a rangoli is one way Indians celebrate their cultural heritage.

REFUGEES OR NOT?

The *Komagata Maru* was the first ship carrying migrants to be turned away from Canada. But it hasn't been the only ship to cause controversy on Canadian shores. In 2010, the MV *Sun Sea* made headlines when it arrived off the west coast with 492 Sri Lankan Tamils aboard. They claimed to be refugees fleeing violence in their country after a prolonged civil war. But Canadian officials suspected the ship was a human smuggling operation—intended to bring people without legal papers across borders—and that many of those on board were linked to terrorist organizations. Authorities kept some of the passengers in detention on shore for almost two years while they carefully investigated each person's background. Anyone suspected of having committed a crime was turned away.

Sri Lankans rally for peace at Parliament Hill in Ottawa, Canada.

7

EXODUS 1947

Ship of Survivors

NAME

First named the *President Warfield* after ship company president S.D. Warfield, it was renamed *Exodus* in 1947 after the Biblical story of the Jewish journey out of Egypt.

FRANCE

ISRAEL

BUILT

In 1928, by Pusey & Jones Corporation in the US state of Delaware.

DESCRIPTION

A steamboat with a capacity of 400, it was formerly a pleasure steamer on the US east coast.

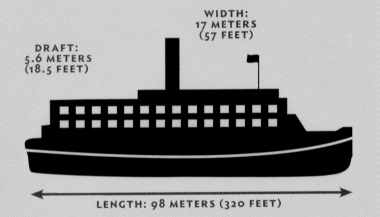

WIDTH:
17 METERS
(57 FEET)

DRAFT:
5.6 METERS
(18.5 FEET)

LENGTH: 98 METERS (320 FEET)

CLAIM TO FAME

The *Exodus 1947* carried around 4,500 Jewish concentration camp survivors—1,600 men, 1,282 women, 1,017 teens and 655 children—to Israel after the Second World War.

WHERE IS IT NOW?

After its historic voyage in 1947, *Exodus* was moored in Haifa, Israel, as a derelict (abandoned) vessel. Plans were made to restore it as a museum, but it burned in 1952. What was left of it was towed to the Bay of Shemen, near Haifa, where it sank. Multiple attempts to raise and salvage it failed. The remains of the hull were visible until 2000, when a container ship quay was built over it.

MEDITERRANEAN SEA [JULY 1947]

Irene leans on the rail at the stern of the Exodus 1947, watching the bubbly wake. It's peaceful on the sea, and if she closes her eyes she can almost imagine away the other 4,500 passengers on this voyage. At least there's fresh air up here on deck, unlike down below. But no one complains. They've finally put the horrors of the concentration camps behind them, and things can only get better.

In the three days since the ship left France, Irene has tried to contain her nervous excitement about what lies ahead. The ceremony to rename the ship Exodus 1947 raised everyone's spirits. Now if this ship can safely reach Palestinian shores, she'll be able to embrace her family again—at least those who are left. Not Papa. She never saw him after that night the Gestapo took him. But Mama, and her sister Monique and little brother Isaac, are waiting for her. For months she hid from the Nazis in the orphanage in Paris, and every day she swore she'd find her family again. It was a miracle to learn they had made it to Palestine. Now it is her turn.

Behind her, some are talking about the inevitable battle to come. Most do not believe the British warships of the Palestine Patrol will let them through the blockade. They could be turned back or sent to Cyprus, where other Jewish immigrants are being held in camps, waiting for their turn to enter Palestine. But if it comes to a fight, Irene doubts their weapons of sticks, potatoes, and cans of food will have much effect against British guns.

The Story of Exodus 1947

THE REMAINS OF THE HULL still lie on the bottom of a bay near Haifa, Israel. Out of sight, but by no means forgotten, *Exodus 1947* will forever be a symbol of a struggle for freedom and identity that spans centuries. That great effort came to a dramatic climax in the summer of 1947, shortly after the Second World War. While the world watched, outraged by the callous treatment of desperate people trying to immigrate to the land they considered theirs, one powerful country barred the way. And a pleasure steamer that began life along the American east coast became embroiled in a deadly incident in the Mediterranean, one that would help to forge a new nation.

Two Visions for Palestine

JEWISH PEOPLE HAVE ALWAYS WISHED to live in Israel, a land they historically claim as sacred through their ancient beliefs. Beginning in the eighth century BCE, they were repeatedly driven from that land at the eastern end of the Mediterranean by different powers. A movement called Zionism arose in the late 19th century urging Jews to return to Israel, so they continued to immigrate there in large numbers. Britain gained the territory after it defeated the Ottoman Empire in the early 1900s. The League of Nations, an organization formed after the First World War to promote peace (and which would later become the United Nations), then gave Britain control of the area known as Palestine, which included Israel. It was to be a home for Jewish people, under the condition that the rights of Arab Muslims and Christians already living there would also be respected. However, the Arab population, which largely outnumbered the Jews, objected to losing what they considered their part of the territory, and began armed attacks in protest.

As more and more Jewish immigrants arrived, Britain struggled to control the hostilities between the cultures. Anxious to be free of this responsibility, in 1939, Britain declared Palestine would be governed jointly by Arabs and Jews. But they imposed a five-year limit to Jewish immigration: 75,000 people. This attempt to appease the Arab population did not sit well with either group. Arabs refused to give up any territory to Jews, who in turn felt they should be able to occupy all of Palestine.

The situation was far from resolved when the Second World War broke out in Europe in 1939. As his armies advanced across Europe, the German Nazi leader, Adolf Hitler, sought to get rid of the entire population of Jews, whom he believed were an inferior race that threatened the German community. Over six million Jews were rounded up, imprisoned, and killed in concentration camps in a brutal program now referred to as the Holocaust.

EXODUS 1947

Women and children at a displaced persons camp in Austria

A New Homeland

LIKE SO MANY PEOPLE DISPLACED by the Second World War in Europe, Jewish survivors of the Holocaust wanted to go back to their homes in 1945, after the war ended. But once they were finally released from concentration camps by the Allies, most found they no longer had homes or businesses to return to—many had been taken over by other people. Immigrating to North America was discouraged by quotas set by the US government. Some went to Australia and South Africa, but the goal for most Jewish survivors was to go to Palestine. They expected to have free access to their spiritual homeland of Israel, even though it was still a British territory. A steady stream of immigrants found their way across the Mediterranean Sea from various European ports. But in the face of Arab opposition, Britain decided not to accept any more Jewish refugees from Europe: in 1946, up to 250,000 people were living in camps for displaced persons in Germany, Austria, and Italy.

Jewish organizations began to plan ways to transport immigrants to Palestine—illegally if necessary. With support from the US and France (since neither country wanted to deal with a large number of immigrants), the organizations found ships and managed to evade the British naval blockade of the Palestine coast. But British vigilance only increased, so many immigrants were redirected to detention camps on Cyprus, an island south of Turkey in the Mediterranean Sea.

Then, in 1947, a confrontation aboard the refugee ship *Exodus 1947* became a flashpoint that gripped the world's attention and focused it sharply on the plight of Jewish Holocaust survivors and their struggle to create their own state.

The Voyage Begins

Exodus 1947 BEGAN LIFE under another name in a different land. Built in America in 1928, the steamer *President Warfield* carried passengers and freight from Baltimore, Maryland, to Norfolk, Virginia, until 1942. Transferred to the British Ministry of War, the *Warfield* became a troop training ship in England. Two years later it narrowly escaped a German U-boat attack, and assisted American soldiers off Normandy during the Allied invasion of Europe. Back in America after the war, the Jewish defense group Haganah saved the vessel from the scrap yard. They planned to refurbish it as a refugee transport ship in the Mediterranean.

One summer night in 1947, the *Warfield* stole out of the harbor at Sète, France. The captain had been given an ultimatum—be out of port by two a.m. or the French, who up until now had been sympathetic to the ship's mission, would block the harbor on orders from England.

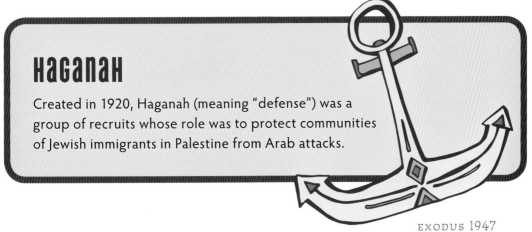

Haganah

Created in 1920, Haganah (meaning "defense") was a group of recruits whose role was to protect communities of Jewish immigrants in Palestine from Arab attacks.

With no pilot to guide it, the ship bumped into docks and ran aground on a sandbar, but managed to find its way to open sea. Its destination: Palestine. But to get there, the *Warfield* would have to dodge British warships watching for it, evade Royal Air Force spotter planes tracking its course, and finally push through any blockade of ships as it neared the Palestinian shore.

The ship, designed for about 400 passengers, was overloaded with over 4,500 Holocaust survivors brought from camps throughout Europe. Everyone on board was prepared to endure the difficult conditions—lineups for the few toilets, rationed water, poor ventilation below decks where sleeping bunks were crammed in as tightly as they had been in the concentration camps. Really, most felt it was nothing compared to what they had suffered in their years of captivity. Now they simply wanted to reach Palestine, expecting to start new lives. Men, women, and children willingly took up cleaning duties and helped to cook and serve meals to keep busy. Classes in Hebrew and lectures about Palestine took their minds off the slow passage of time during the weeklong journey.

Jewish immigrants aboard *Exodus 1947*

A New Name Brings Hope

On the second day out, the Haganah leaders renamed the ship *Exodus 1947*, and hope filled the air. The word *exodus* means "a journey taken by a large group to escape from a hostile environment." It comes from a story in the Old Testament about Moses leading Israelites out of Egypt. The new name was printed on a large banner and hung in plain view on the ship.

The crew prepared for trouble by posting lookouts on the bridge. At night, they ran the ship without lights and as quietly as possible. Lifeboats and rafts were stocked with supplies. All those capable of fighting had been organized into a defensive force and shown how to use the weapons at hand: no guns, but a supply of potatoes and food cans to throw as missiles, hammers and other small tools for hand-to-hand combat, and even boiling water from the galley, if needed, to throw on attackers. Hoses had been rigged from the engine room to spray oil on the deck, which would make boarding the ship tough, and barbed wire was strung around the decks. The passengers of *Exodus 1947* were determined to reach their destination at all costs.

But the British were equally determined to stop this blockade runner (a ship that tries to reach shore illegally), even though stopping the ship outside Palestinian territorial waters was against maritime law (no single country rules international waters). British soldiers were equipped with submachine guns, clubs, and axes, and some carried battering rams to break down cabin doors on *Exodus 1947*. Expecting strong opposition, they wore helmets, and gas masks to protect themselves from the tear gas they would use to subdue the passengers and crew.

SS *PRESIDENT WARFIELD'S* ALMOST-ROYAL CONNECTION

Before it became *Exodus 1947*, the *Warfield* was named for the president of an American shipping company. But his niece was much better known. Wallis Simpson became the Duchess of Windsor in 1936 when Edward, who was destined to be King Edward VIII of England, gave up his claim to the throne so that he could marry Simpson, a divorced commoner.

The Battle

Just before midnight on July 17, brilliant search lights suddenly beamed from a British warship—part of the Palestine Patrol, responsible for blockading the ports. *Exodus 1947* was commanded to change course and proceed under escort. Instead, the refugee ship held its steady pace. The captain knew a spurt of speed once they were closer to shore would bring the risk of grounding the ship, although everyone felt losing the ship that way would be better than surrendering.

In the darkness, five destroyers and one cruiser closed in around *Exodus 1947*. The captain ordered his ship to increase its speed toward the Egyptian coast, now only 27 kilometers (17 miles) away. They would try to hug the coastline, hopefully in water too shallow for the warships to get close enough to board. Once as near to the Palestinian beaches as possible, the passengers could be sent out in lifeboats and rafts. It would be dangerous as British troops and tanks would resist any landing attempts.

Dawn approached as *Exodus 1947* neared the shore. Politicians and journalists, drawn by news of the unfolding drama, gathered on shore for a clear view of any conflict. How would the world react to the story of these refugees whose wish to go to Palestine was so strong that they would risk their lives?

A Dark and Dangerous Time

As THE WARSHIPS DREW UP ALONGSIDE, the captain of *Exodus 1947* ordered "reverse engines" in a final attempt to dodge the boarding party. The warships began to ram *Exodus 1947*, trying to force it to stop. The assault was on! Soldiers pelted with potatoes and food cans hurled by passengers took shelter in cabins. Others had to break through barbed wire around the wheelhouse to take control of the ship. Firecrackers mimicking gunshots were going off everywhere and choking tear gas drifted across the deck, made slick with oil. *Exodus 1947* put on full speed, hoping to remain in the safety of international waters.

For over four hours, passengers and crew kept up a valiant struggle, while doctors on board attempted to treat the wounded. Even though three people had already been killed and nearly 200 injured, the captain still wouldn't give in. But eventually, when the condition of several badly injured crew members and passengers became critical, he was forced to ask for medical aid to prevent further loss of life.

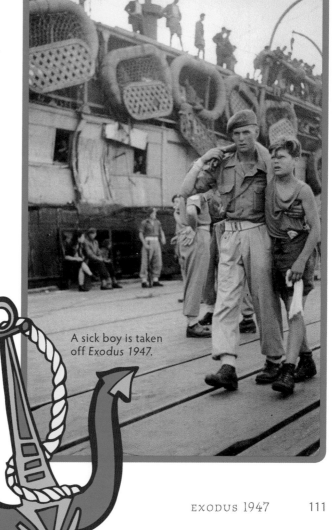

A sick boy is taken off *Exodus 1947*.

Defeat, but Not Surrender

BATTERED AND BRUISED, *Exodus 1947* limped into the harbor at Haifa under heavy guard. But it was not the homecoming the passengers had wished for and fought so hard to achieve. Instead of being allowed to stay ashore, all but the most seriously injured were rushed aboard three British transport ships waiting to take them back to France. The British, embarrassed by the whole affair, chose to ignore criticism. In spite of a huge gathering of reporters from around the world, no one was allowed to talk to the refugees about the confrontation. When the ships were loaded, they sailed back to the French port from which *Exodus 1947* had embarked only a few days before.

But that was not the end of their journey either. Once again, French authorities were prepared to help, but the passengers refused to leave the ship. Britain wanted to use force to unload them; France resisted. After a standoff and hunger strike that lasted about a month, the ships and all passengers aboard were sent to Hamburg, Germany. Imagine how terrible it must have been for those Holocaust survivors to be returned to the country that had imprisoned them and torn apart their families. In fact, they were taken by train to camps much like the ones they'd left, though in a part of Germany now occupied by Britain.

Passengers from *Exodus 1947* disembark from a train in Hamburg as British soldiers watch.

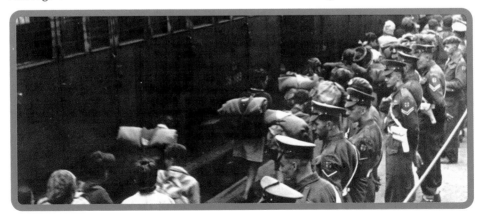

FROM ONE PRISON TO ANOTHER

For a time, the small Mediterranean island of Cyprus became just another prison for up to 53,000 Jewish survivors of Nazi concentration camps. After the Second World War ended, Jews trying to reach Palestine ran into immigration limitations imposed by Britain. The British government decided to hold the overflow of refugees in internment camps in Cyprus, which at the time was a British crown colony. Most couldn't complete the journey they'd begun until the State of Israel was created by the United Nations in 1948.

The Legacy

THE INTERNATIONAL OUTCRY GREW LOUDER and Britain became the object of worldwide shame for its treatment of the refugees. Jewish organizations pushed harder for the creation of Israel as a destination for all Jewish war victims stranded in displaced-person camps in Europe. It took almost another year before the UN voted to divide Palestine and officially create the State of Israel. The last of the *Exodus 1947* refugees set foot in that homeland in June 1948.

The re-purposed steamboat may have failed to deliver its cargo as planned, but the war-weary world recognized the attempt as a symbol of the struggle against oppression. For the Jewish people, the story of *Exodus 1947* and its courageous passengers and crew inspired a decisive change, and represents the hope of finding a compromise that all nations in the region can live with.

8

GRANMA

Launching a Revolution

NAME
The ship is believed to be named after
the original owner's grandmother.

MEXICO

TUXPAN

CUBA

PLAYA LAS COLORADAS

BUILT

In 1938 in the US; purchased by a Mexican supporter of Fidel Castro in October 1956 for $15,000 USD.

DESCRIPTION

An American leisure yacht with two diesel-powered engines and a capacity of 12.

LENGTH: 21 METERS (68 FEET)

CLAIM TO FAME

The *Granma* carried a group of revolutionaries—including Fidel Castro—to Cuba in 1956. Its secretive and stormy voyage became a symbol of Cuba's determined struggle for freedom from both an oppressive dictator and US control of its economy.

WHERE IS IT NOW?

The *Granma* was transferred to Havana Bay in 1959. Since 1976, it has been on display in a bulletproof glass enclosure next to the Museum of the Revolution in Havana.

CUBA
[July 26, 1953]

Antonio crouches by his open bedroom window, peering through the early morning mist. All is quiet, and he knows he probably won't be able to hear any gunfire. It has been a couple of hours since his father and older brothers left in the predawn darkness, driving to a secret gathering place nearby. Antonio wishes he could have gone too. Instead, he and his mother can only wait for them to return. The damp air, or maybe the thought of the danger the men will be in today, makes him shiver.

So much planning, so many late night meetings...Antonio secretly listened to his father and other men sitting around their kitchen table talking. He knows they are angry with the president, Batista, who canceled last year's election and took power without letting ordinary Cubans have their say. Now the man they wanted to elect to the Congress to speak for them will have no chance. His father and the others look to Fidel Castro as a bold leader willing to challenge Batista and Antonio overheard his father say that this morning's planned attack will be the start of an uprising across the island. Those who support this revolution see it as the only way to force Batista from office. But will it work?

Antonio's father says he's too young to be fighting this battle. But if it's successful, it could mean big changes for his family and the entire country—and he wants to be a part of it! Surely his family will be better off if Cuba is free from the control of an oppressive ruler! Will there be more jobs if Cubans can take back ownership of sugar plantations from the Americans? There are plenty of riches in the city, but little for peasant families like Antonio's. He would be proud to see his country become truly independent. But first, his father and the other men must return home safely from this daring assault.

A replica of the *Granma* in a 2011 parade in Havana, Cuba

The Story of the Granma

"MAN OVERBOARD!"

The cry arose on a stormy November night in the Caribbean. A man had climbed onto the cabin of a small yacht, the *Granma*, trying to spot a landmark—the lighthouse at Cabo Cruz on the southern tip of Cuba—but lost his footing. His comrades-in-arms on board had no choice but to stop and search for him. But the darkness and wild waves made it almost impossible to follow his faint cries for help. Their leader, Fidel Castro, refused to give up, even using a searchlight, putting them at greater risk of being spotted. At last, the man was pulled, exhausted, from the water.

THE OTHER GRANMA

Granma is also a daily newspaper, named after the yacht Castro sailed to Cuba in 1956. It was established in 1965 and is the official newspaper of the ruling Communist Party.

Who were these men, what were they doing out on the choppy waters that night, and why had they risked their lives in such a perilous bid to reach their homeland? Their voyage was a rough beginning for a course that would change the face of their own country and have a serious impact on others.

It was November 25, 1956. The crossing of the *Granma* from Mexico to Cuba was part of a grand plan to ignite a smoldering revolutionary fire. On board were 81 followers of a man whose mission was to rid his island nation of a cruel dictator and the heavy hand of American control. Years of strife had brought Fidel Castro and the rebels to this point. It would mean yet another battle in the long, troubled history of Cuba. But this one, unlike others in the past, had the greatest chance of success because of the doggedness of its leaders.

Ruled from Afar

Cuba's story began long before this particular voyage. Over four centuries earlier, Christopher Columbus had sailed to the West Indies seeking a route to the East for spices. He reported back to the king of Spain that the climate and soil of islands such as Cuba were perfect for growing sugar. The Spanish quickly set up plantations, using indigenous people as workers. They suffered under cruel working conditions and were soon wiped out by European diseases like smallpox. So African slaves were then brought by the hundreds of thousands as labor for the booming sugar industry.

The Iznaga Tower served as a lookout for supervising sugar plantation slaves.

This practice continued for 300 years and Cuba's populations of both white Spanish immigrants and black Africans grew. Wealthy Spanish plantation owners dominated the sugar market, but locally born white Cubans also profited in the colony until slavery was abolished in the mid-1800s.

Meanwhile, money had been flowing into Cuba as Americans bought up the sugar business, creating bigger, modernized companies. Smaller Cuban operations lost their share of the market. Amid growing discontent, the first Cuban War of Independence against Spain broke out in 1868. It failed after a 10-year struggle, and about one third of the wealthier population moved to the United States. But the spark had been lit: could Cubans now settle for less than liberty?

Independence . . . for a Price

BUT CUBANS WOULD NOT HAVE THEIR FREEDOM . . . yet. Spain clamped down even harder, imposing high taxes and giving Cubans no say in their government. Already completely dependent on American money for its only crop, sugar, Cuba feared even greater control as the US began to raise fees for sugar imports. Cuba's second attempt to gain its independence erupted in 1895, prompting the US government to step in to protect its sugar operations. Cubans' own wishes were lost amid the conflict between the larger warring nations in the Spanish–American War.

When the dust settled, Cuba was finally rid of Spain, but now had a new master: the United States. After a military occupation of Cuba on and off for eight years, the US allowed the country to become a republic and to elect its own government. But there were conditions. While it withdrew its soldiers, the US kept military bases in Cuba and retained the right to use force to keep order. It also still controlled Cuba's business dealings with other countries.

The island's troubles were far from over. It may have been independent in name since 1902, but a succession of corrupt leaders supported by the US continued to fuel unrest. The last of these, Fulgencio Batista, held power as a dictator while Cuba's economy suffered first from dropping prices for sugar after the First World War, and then, along with the rest of the world, from the Great Depression beginning in 1929. Ordinary Cuban citizens grew more and more impatient for real independence and equality.

Batista visiting Washington, DC, in 1938

A graffiti portrait in Havana celebrates Castro (center) and Che Guevara (right).

Changes in the Wind

In 1945, a law student at the University of Havana emerged as a strong voice against governmental cruelty and lawlessness, and American control of Cuba's industries. Fidel Castro was so passionate about the need for Cuban self-rule that he tried to run for election in 1952. Batista canceled the elections, though, and in response Castro lead fellow revolutionaries in an attack on the army barracks to seize weapons. He was captured and jailed until 1955, when he fled to Mexico. He spent the next couple of years organizing and training a band of guerillas—armed citizens using military tactics—called the July 26 Movement. Named for the date of that failed 1953 attack that had signaled the beginning of a revolution, the group, which included Castro's brother, Raúl, drew in another ardent supporter of the cause,

Che Guevara. These rebels felt it was their duty—their passion—to lead their nation to independence, and no sacrifice was too much.

That's why, in the early morning hours of November 25, 1956, the rebels—who had left training camps scattered throughout Mexico—gathered in silence under cover of darkness, amid driving rain. Their stealth was crucial to avoiding detection by Mexican police, the FBI, or agents of Batista, all of whom constantly harassed them. Castro had raised money to buy a 20-meter (65-foot) yacht, the *Granma*, but it was far from ideal. More than 20 years old, it had two engines in desperate need of repair, and its radio could receive but not send signals. There would be no way to tell their comrades waiting on Cuba's shore about their progress. Their aim was to arrive in five days' time to support attacks planned to begin on November 30. In order to make the 1,987-kilometer (1,235-mile) crossing of the Gulf of Mexico (about the same distance as from Seattle, WA, to San Diego, CA), extra fuel had to be stored in drums on deck. That cut down the already limited space for the 82 men and their weapons and ammunition in a boat built to carry only 12. No wonder the boat came close to foundering in the stormy seas that night.

Che Guevara (1928–1967)

Ernesto (Che) Guevara, a doctor from Argentina and an activist against inequality and poverty, became a comrade of Fidel Castro in Mexico and participated in the Cuban Revolution. His brutal treatment of opponents of Castro's government painted him as a radical in the eyes of the world. As Castro's right-hand man, he encouraged Cuba's close alliance with the Soviet Union in taking a stand against the US. In his roles as Minister of Industry and president of the Bank of Cuba, he pushed for reforms to help those living in poverty. Guevara was killed in Bolivia fighting for his communist beliefs, and has become a symbol of rebellion to many. His legend is kept alive by his facial image, with dark, curly hair and a beret, often seen on posters and T-shirts.

The Voyage Begins

GRANMA CREPT OUT OF THE MEXICAN PORT of Tuxpan at two a.m. without lights. As soon as it cleared the coast, seasickness hit many on board. Castro had been warned of bad weather, but could not delay the departure—he was a wanted man. The dangerously overloaded boat lurched through the waves, chugging at a snail's pace across the open water, past the Yucatán Peninsula, past the Cayman Islands. Far slower than expected! To make matters worse, one engine failed and *Granma* began to leak. They bailed. They ran out of food and fresh water. Only the momentous news on the radio that the revolution had begun in eastern Cuba—without them—fired their spirits. But they were impatient, and the frantic search for the man who had fallen overboard delayed them even more.

Out of fuel after seven days, *Granma* finally ran aground in a mangrove swamp on Cuba's southern coast. Now the desperate, exhausted men had to thrash their way through tangled branches and soft mud the width of a football field to reach shore. It was impossible to take their weapons. By daylight, they were still straggling ashore, fearful of the government patrol planes they knew would easily spot them in the open if word was out about their arrival. They sought help from friendly occupants of a small house, just in time. Planes appeared and began to fire on the stranded *Granma*. For days, Castro's rebels dodged ambushes and were forced to hide in the countryside. The glorious arrival they planned had gone completely awry, and in the end only 21 of the group made it to a safe hideout in the Sierra Maestra Mountains.

The *Granma* on a 1996 stamp

A 1976 stamp commemorating the 20th anniversary of the Cuban Revolution

The Revolution

In the months that followed, the rural-based guerillas and urban fighters regrouped to push forward the Cuban Revolution and win rule "by the people." After Batista fled, stealing millions of dollars, Castro became prime minister, and later president. He quickly initiated a government takeover of many large American-owned industries, including sugar plantations and refineries. He tolerated no opposition, imprisoning or executing many who challenged him. But his ideal of *Cuba libre* (a free Cuba) was extremely popular among the people.

The US government became alarmed as it saw its grip on Cuba threatened. It reduced trade, trying to stir up Cuban citizens against their new leaders. Soon the two governments were no longer speaking to each other. Then Cuba turned to America's Cold War enemy—the Soviet Union—and became a trading partner for sugar in exchange for

Castro visiting
Washington, DC,
in 1959

oil. Castro declared Cuba a socialist country. Cubans living in the States showed their resentment of the new order by planning an invasion at the Bay of Pigs in 1962, backed by American President John F. Kennedy. But due to Castro's strength and the fierce loyalty of his people, the attack failed and only intensified Castro's hatred of America. In a belligerent move, he urged the Soviet Union to secretly place nuclear weapons and troops in Cuba as a defense against another suspected attack by Americans.

COLD WAR

In the Second World War, America and the Soviet Union were allies against a common enemy, Germany. But after that war, tension between the countries simmered for over 40 years, a period known as the Cold War. Though there was no open conflict between these superpowers, their distrust of each other fostered a fear of nuclear war that led each nation to build up defensive weapons. Both sides also competed to gain influence over smaller countries around the world. But the most serious flashpoint was the Cuban missile crisis of 1962, when nuclear war was narrowly avoided. The Cold War thawed after the collapse of the Soviet Union in 1991.

A Standoff

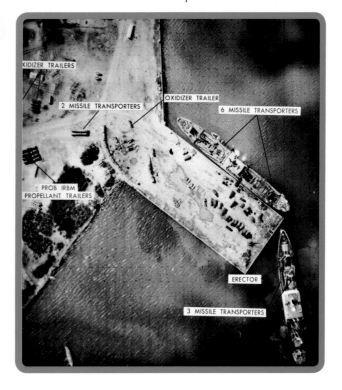

FOR 13 DAYS IN OCTOBER, 1962, the world held its breath as the Cuban missile crisis unfolded. Never before had such a grave threat of nuclear war faced North America on its very doorstep. The US Navy rushed to block ships from the Soviet Union bringing more nuclear weapons to Cuba. Which nation would blink first?

Thankfully, the Soviet leaders, without consulting Castro, reached an agreement with the US to withdraw their missiles and troops. The world could breathe again. But could Cuban leaders still trust their communist ally? Officials in Moscow and Washington realized how close they'd come to a devastating war. One of the things they did to help ward off any future incidents that might spiral out of control was set up a direct telephone "hotline" between the two nations.

Following the crisis, the US ended all trade with Cuba. Now Cuba was isolated, except for economic help from the Soviets. During the 1970s and 1980s Castro worked to build his country by creating a new constitution, and establishing free education and health programs. When the Soviet Union broke up in 1991, that source of money dried up. Despite an American trade blockade for over 50 years, and ongoing issues of poverty and food rationing, Cuba has continued as an independent nation, deeply committed to its freedom. Its leader, Fidel Castro, never gave in to political and economic pressures as its nearest neighbor, the US, always expected he would.

MARIEL BOATLIFT

In 1980, small boats played another key role in Cuba's history. A flotilla of boats transported almost 125,000 Cubans to Florida. Before then, Cuban borders had been mostly closed. But a period of closer relations with America prompted Castro to allow some travel in and out of the country. A few residents, dissatisfied with Cuba's weak economy, saw a chance to ask Peru to accept them as refugees. This opened the floodgates; up to 10,000 gathered at Peru's embassy in Havana. Castro then decided to allow anyone who wanted to leave Cuba to do so, but they had to find their own way from the port of Mariel. In Florida, Cuban Americans rounded up as many small boats as they could find and sailed to the island to pick up people. The operation, called the Mariel boatlift, continued from April to October. Overcrowded boats were helped by the US Coast Guard, and airplane hangars in Miami became temporary camps to process the unexpected flood of people.

What's Next for Cuba?

Today Cuba's economy depends on new industries including medicine, tourism, and nickel mining. It has a growing organic agriculture sector, producing food on small farms and city plots, and is investing in energy sources like wind and solar power. Almost everyone in Cuba's population of 11 million can read and write. New agreements with Brazil and European countries promise trade opportunities. And in January 2015, Cuba and the US held diplomatic talks—their first step toward better relations in over 50 years.

Despite these optimistic signs, Cuba is still tightly controlled by its single political party. Its government restricts any opposition and limits freedoms such as travel outside Cuba and access to the Internet. Only recently have people been allowed to buy and sell their own homes and cars, and they can only invest in small businesses.

Fidel Castro stepped aside as president in 2008 at age 82. His successor, his brother Raúl, has taken a more moderate view of the goals of the revolutionaries, set in motion that night aboard the *Granma,* whose stormy passage reflects Cuba's dramatic history.

9

RAINBOW WARRIOR

Flagship of Protest

NAME

Believed to have come from an indigenous myth about people called Warriors of the Rainbow, who would one day gather to act against human threats to nature.

ALASKA

AMCHITKA

GERMANY

BANGLADESH
CHITTAGONG

NEW ZEALAND

BUILT

Rainbow Warrior I in Scotland in 1955 as a fishing trawler named *Sir William Hardy,* bought by the environmental group Greenpeace and relaunched in 1978 after refitting; *II* in England in 1957, from the hull of a deep-sea fishing ship, relaunched after refitting in 1989; *III* from scratch in Germany in 2011, at a cost of $32 million.

DESCRIPTION

Three ships have sailed under the name *Rainbow Warrior. I:* a fishing trawler; *II:* a steam-powered three-masted schooner (or sailing ship); and *III,* a custom-built eco-friendly yacht.

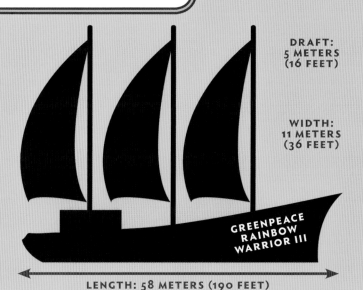

DRAFT:
5 METERS
(16 FEET)

WIDTH:
11 METERS
(36 FEET)

GREENPEACE
RAINBOW
WARRIOR III

LENGTH: 58 METERS (190 FEET)

CLAIM TO FAME

Since the 1970s, Greenpeace's three *Rainbow Warrior* ships have played important roles in the environmental movement, drawing attention to global issues including nuclear testing, overfishing of endangered species, and pollution.

WHERE ARE THEY NOW?

I: sunk July 10, 1985, in New Zealand, and towed to Matauri Bay for use as an artificial diving reef; *II:* retired in 2011 and donated for use as a floating hospital in Bangladesh, now called *Rongdhonu;* *III:* launched in 2011 and currently active.

NEAR KAOSHIUNG, TAIWAN [2011]

The waves look rough, and Melanie is fighting the stirrings of seasickness. "Keep your eyes on the horizon" is the advice of the crew on Rainbow Warrior II. It's only Melanie's third excursion on the ship, this time on a tour of East Asia. Since helping to raise and release salmon fry at a British Columbia hatchery, she's been passionate about protecting marine life, and she's excited to promote this mission's goal: creating a network of marine reserves in the world's oceans.

Today the ship is on its way to a port in Taiwan, where the Greenpeace crew plans to block a tuna factory ship from sailing. Melanie has studied the alarming decline in the tuna population from overfishing, and knows they need to send Taiwan a message. She'll just have to put up with feeling seasick; it's part of the job.

She's heard the crew talk about the big refrigerated factory ships, sometimes known to smuggle huge catches of fish by transferring them at sea to smaller vessels. This ship was caught several years ago for illegal fishing. Now Greenpeace has learned that it is not even legally registered in Taiwan, a fact they'll use to try to stop it from leaving the port. Their strategy is risky. A protester will lock herself to the anchor chain, fully expecting to be arrested by port authorities. But while the ship is delayed to sort this out, the organization will demand that Taiwanese officials investigate the ship's registration issues.

The skyline of Kaoshiung is getting closer. The sight of land is welcome news for Melanie's upset stomach. It isn't her turn to be front and center in this protest. Still, she's anxious about what lies ahead.

The Story of Rainbow Warrior

THE BRIGHT-GREEN SCHOONER with its tall, white sails slips quietly into the port. The dove and rainbow insignia on the hull marks the *Rainbow Warrior* as belonging to the activist group Greenpeace. This ship, newly built in 2011, has a history that stretches way back to the 1970s. That's when an ambitious idea became reality—a group of protesters wanted a way to reach the scenes of activities they considered harmful to the planet. Now with many sea miles and a long list of projects behind it, and a good deal of controversy in its wake, *Rainbow Warrior* has had a significant impact on the way people think about nature.

The name *Rainbow Warrior* is well known around the world. Three ships have sailed under this same name as the flagship of Greenpeace, a prominent organization in the environmental movement. The first two were older ships bought and refitted by Greenpeace to carry out its global campaigns. But the third and latest *Rainbow Warrior* was specially designed and built as a vessel for both environmental operations and scientific expeditions. These three ships have transported activists to locations worldwide to raise awareness and change attitudes about the harm human activities do to the natural environment. Whether the issue is global warming, deforestation, overfishing, seal hunting, whaling, toxic-waste dumping, oil drilling, or nuclear testing, you can count on *Rainbow Warrior* to be on the spot attracting media attention. The group first took to the seas in 1971 to protest the testing of a nuclear bomb in Alaska. Such specific actions to show dissent may seem commonplace today, but the seeds of the environmental movement—a powerful social revolution—had been sown centuries ago.

A Wealth of Resources for All

In the 1600s, Europeans arrived on North American shores and immediately began settling the wild lands they found. They made free use of the trees, water, and wildlife. Why not, when these resources seemed endless and abundant? With the Industrial Revolution in the 1800s, factories used even more raw materials and created the first serious pollution of air and water. Settlers moved farther and farther west, looking for new wood supplies as forests were cleared.

Before long, some people realized the natural world could not go on supplying them forever. For instance, they saw how bison and passenger pigeons were disappearing because of overhunting. In fact, passenger pigeons have been extinct since 1914, and the bison that remain today are mostly kept in small, domestic herds. Some thinkers, writers, and artists began to express concerns about these threats in their work. They tried to promote the idea of living more in harmony with nature by urging governments to set aside land in parks where plants and animals would be protected and preserved. But some politicians and

An 1860 illustration shows forests cut down to make way for houses in California

businesspeople felt that any resource—even within those parks—should be used, as long as limits were set. Contrasting ideas about conservation became flashpoints for disagreement. Some people said that predators, such as wolves, played a crucial role in nature. This seemed ridiculous to others, who felt these species were simply dangerous, and best hunted out of existence.

These matters were left unresolved when the world's attention was pulled away by the First and Second World Wars. Only after the wars, with an explosion in the demand for cars, and the increasing use of chemicals to create plastics and pesticides, did the effects of human activities on nature begin to hit the headlines again.

HOW WE TALK ABOUT THE ENVIRONMENT

ECOLOGY: The relationship of living things to each other, and to what's around them

ECOSYSTEM: A community of living things within a habitat where each part depends on the others

FOOD CHAIN: The flow of energy between living things as animals eat plants or one another

Warnings!

Iℕ the postwar 1950s and 1960s, a growing population of young people became aware of the destructive effects of nuclear weapons, like those used to gain Japan's surrender in the Second World War, and the mounting problems of pollution. Examples were shocking. The blasts that decimated the Japanese cities of Hiroshima and Nagasaki killed over 200,000 outright, and radiation sickness would go on killing thousands more for decades. In 1967, the catastrophic oil spill from the tanker ship *Torrey Canyon* contaminated the coast of England. Widespread mercury poisoning from plastics production entered the food chain of a town called Minamata in Japan, causing people to experience damage to their vision, hearing, and speech, and even severe paralysis. Then evidence came to light in North America that a chemical pesticide called DDT was wiping out not only harmful insects but many beneficial species, including birds and fish.

Within this atmosphere of anxiety in the late 1960s—not only about pollution, but also about the threat of devastating nuclear war—the environmental movement took off, and Greenpeace stepped into the limelight. It started out in Vancouver, British Columbia, as a small peace group called Don't Make a Wave. They began to make headlines with demonstrations and meetings intended to spread environmental information to students, activists, and other interested groups. Wanting to speak out against the spread of nuclear weapons, they set their sights on Amchitka, one of the Aleutian Islands, near Alaska. After the US tested an underground nuclear bomb at Amchitka in 1965, scientists detected radiation far from ground zero. Protesters feared another blast so close to a major fault line—and the location of previous quakes—could trigger an earthquake and tsunami. It would damage habitats and kill wildlife in what was mostly a nature refuge area.

The next test went ahead in 1969, despite demonstrations. As feared, the blast dried up lakes and killed wildlife. Alarm grew as a third test was planned for 1971, this time with a larger, 5-megaton bomb.

VOICES THAT INSPIRED THE ENVIRONMENTAL MOVEMENT

RALPH WALDO EMERSON (1803–1882), in his book *Nature*, expressed his view of the way an appreciation of nature influences one's faith.

HENRY DAVID THOREAU (1817–1862), in *Walden*, a collection of essays, showed how threats to the natural world also affect humans, and encouraged the preservation of wild places.

JOHN MUIR (1838–1914), naturalist and author of *Our National Parks*, stressed the value of keeping wilderness intact, rather than just conserving it by the wise use of natural resources.

ALDO LEOPOLD (1887–1948), in his book *A Sand County Almanac*, focused on seeing the harmony that exists between the land, nature, and humans.

RACHEL CARSON (1907–1964), with her bestselling but controversial book *Silent Spring*, revealed the deadly impact of DDT in food chains. The chemical is now banned in agriculture in many places, though it is an effective control for insects causing typhus and malaria, and is still used in some developing countries.

Although the activists were stopped before reaching Amchitka, they captured the world's attention.

Time to Act

WHAT COULD A SMALL PEACE GROUP do almost 4,000 kilometers (2,400 miles) away in Vancouver? How could they join protesters near the site? Determined, they rented a boat, hired its captain, and battled stormy seas and the threat of arrest by US authorities to try to reach Amchitka. Unfortunately, they were stopped by the US Coast Guard before they even got close. But their journey caught the attention of a few journalists and the story created a media frenzy. Despite growing disapproval from Canadian and Japanese officials, scientists, and concerned citizens across North America, the test went ahead. Once again, the explosion caused substantial damage to the land and wildlife. The public outcry was so great that the Americans then abandoned testing. But the protest group, now known as Greenpeace—*green* for its environmental focus and *peace* for its original vision—had found its mission. Its founders knew direct action would make the world sit up and take notice of environmental issues.

Now what they needed was a reliable way to get to where the action was: Greenpeace wanted its own ship. It launched fundraising campaigns to buy a used fishery research trawler. After a refit and a new name, the *Rainbow Warrior* headed to Iceland in 1978 to protest commercial whaling. Unwelcome in a country where so many earned a living from the sea, the activists faced armed opposition from whalers as they disrupted the hunt and published photos and stories about declining whale populations. The whaling protest was a dangerous and ambitious undertaking, but it helped to keep the topic of whaling on the front pages long enough for some countries to declare a partial ban four years later.

In the Pacific Ocean in 1985, Greenpeace used the *Rainbow Warrior* to relocate 320 residents from an atoll—a coral reef encircling a lagoon— that had been contaminated by American nuclear tests in the 1950s, taking them to the Marshall Islands, northeast of the Philippines. Later that year, they tied the ship up in the harbor at Auckland, New Zealand, preparing to lead a convoy of protest vessels to the uninhabited French colony of Moruroa, north of Tahiti. The French government had been using Moruroa Atoll for nuclear testing since the 1960s. Greenpeace had already brought media attention to the issue, trying to stop further tests for fear of radioactive contamination. Now they had concerns about the long-term harm to the coral island and its marine life, and to people living on nearby atolls.

But on July 10, 1985, before the *Rainbow Warrior* could set sail as planned, two bomb blasts ripped its hull apart. One man, a photographer, was killed. When it was discovered that French government agents had planted the bombs, protests erupted around the world, sparking trade boycotts of French products. Attempts to salvage the ship failed, and it was towed to a nearby island and sunk to become an artificial diving reef.

WRECKS AS DIVING REEFS

Rainbow Warrior I, once home to environmental activists, now rests on the ocean floor in Matauri Bay, New Zealand. Deliberately sunk there in 1987 after it was destroyed by bombs two years earlier, it provides a dive site for scuba divers as well as a home for marine creatures and plants. Many ships retired from service for various reasons are sunk to create these artificial reefs. They are first cleaned of all oils and chemicals that would cause pollution, and stripped of parts that might collapse once corrosion from salt water sets in. Extra openings cut in the hull allow divers to safely enter and exit the wreck as they explore it. *Rainbow Warrior*, defender of nature on the sea, is now giving shelter to the natural world beneath it.

A snorkeler explores the wreck of the USAT *Liberty* off the island of Bali in Indonesia.

A New Ship, New Campaigns

T HE FIRST RAINBOW WARRIOR WAS GONE, but its loss had raised awareness about a problem that would occur again. France resumed tests in Moruroa Atoll in the 1990s. By then, Greenpeace had launched *Rainbow Warrior II*, a refitted three-masted schooner. It planned to collect plankton samples near the atoll to test for radioactivity. The story made headlines when the French government again blocked their attempts to approach the area, and seized the ship. Greenpeace sued the government for violating its civil rights and freedoms, and for the cost of damages.

In other campaigns, *Rainbow Warrior II* focused on drift nets, which often wastefully kill sea creatures that fishing boats aren't trying to catch. *Rainbow Warrior II* was on site to record the ruinous effects of the oil spill left by the tanker *Exxon Valdez* near Alaska in 1991. Off the coast of Spain, it took part in protests against England's dumping of radioactive and industrial waste at sea. And it took activists into the media spotlight at international conferences where powerful leaders were meeting to discuss issues like deforestation and climate change.

HARMONY WITH NATURE

In addition to the dove and rainbow insignia on the hull, the *Rainbow Warrior* ships also display a circular image on the funnel (chimney) showing two whales, symbolizing harmony with nature. The design was offered to Greenpeace by the Kwakwaka'wakw people of the Pacific Northwest Coast at the time of the group's first campaign to Amchitka.

During its 22 years of service, *Rainbow Warrior II* became an even more visible symbol of Greenpeace as video technology allowed the world to see exactly what the activists were doing, often in real time. Their preferred tactic of direct but nonviolent action might mean locking themselves to anchor chains, scaling huge smokestacks to hang banners, or standing on ice floes between armed seal hunters and their prey. These images became well known worldwide. So did the inflatable rubber boats, a big part of Greenpeace's protest methods since they were first carried aboard *Rainbow Warrior I* in 1975. Zooming around whaling ships between the whales and ready-to-fire harpoons, or charging in front of cargo ships carrying rare types of wood from endangered tree species, these activists appear to be ready to do anything to interfere with the progress of activities they oppose.

Greenpeace's giant polar bear, Aurora, parades through London to draw attention to the effects of Arctic oil drilling on wildlife.

What Has Changed?

GREENPEACE'S PROTESTS HAVE DRAWN both positive and negative reactions. Some people see their actions as radical, foolhardy, and dangerous, accomplishing little more than generating sensational media coverage. But with a membership that has grown to almost 3 million, in over 40 countries, clearly others see these actions as a necessary way of bringing crucial issues to the forefront: that threatened populations of whales are being hunted, for example, or that rainforests are being destroyed by illegal harvesting. Can dramatic acts create a better understanding of these problems? As a result of campaigns aboard *Rainbow Warrior II*, Greenpeace claims some credit for agreements that have reduced the impact of overfishing of tuna, clear-cut logging, hunting of seal pups, salmon farming, and Arctic oil drilling, among other issues. Whether you agree or not with Greenpeace's protest methods, it's clear that the *Rainbow Warrior* has been a major tool in helping to spark discussion, debate, and even considerable shifts in our thoughts and actions toward the environment.

The Future of the Rainbow Warrior

In 2011, a new Rainbow Warrior was designed and built, using funds mainly donated from individuals, rather than political parties or companies that might influence Greenpeace's decisions. The new ship once again wears the trademark bright green of the organization, symbolizing its mission to focus on solutions to global environmental problems. Respecting such goals, the ship makes use of environmentally friendly technology: sails to use wind energy, recycled water and engine heat, fuel conservation, and high-tech navigation and communication systems. Capable of launching small inflatable craft and even fitted with a helicopter pad, *Rainbow Warrior III* will continue the work begun in 1971, reminding the world of the potential damage of the human footprint in the natural world.

Earth Day

In 1970, the first Earth Day was held throughout the US as an event to spread the message about "green" issues. The brainchild of US Senator Gaylord Nelson, it caught on among the many protest groups targeting various environmental problems across America. Suddenly it became clear that they all had similar goals. Why not work together to create a louder voice? A tradition began: now, in 180 countries around the world, every April 22 is declared Earth Day.

10

SIRIUS & STAR

Somali Pirate Prize

NAME

Sirius Star was owned by Saudi Aramco and operated by Vela International's company called Star Enterprises. All ships operated by Vela International are named for stars in the Vela (Latin for "sails") constellation, found in the southern sky. Sirius is one of those stars.

AFRICA

SOMALIA
KENYA

TANZANIA

● SIRIUS STAR HIJACKING

MADAGASCAR

BUILT

In 2008,
South Korea

DESCRIPTION

Known as a VLCC—Very Large
Crude (Oil) Carrier. A flag of
convenience ship registered in
Liberia, its home port is Monrovia.

CLAIM TO FAME

In 2008, *Sirius Star* was
carrying 2 million
barrels of crude oil from
Saudi Arabia (with a
value of $100 million) to a
US port in the Caribbean
when it was hijacked by
Somali pirates, causing
international ripples and
drawing attention to the
poverty and desperation
of East Africans.

WEIGHT:
330,000
TONS

DRAFT:
12 METERS
(72 FEET)

WIDTH:
58 METERS
(190 FEET)

LENGTH: 330 METERS (1,080 FEET)

WHERE IS IT NOW?

The ship is still active, but has been renamed
Manifa and is now owned by the National Shipping
Company of Saudi Arabia. For its current location,
go to www.fleetmon.com/en/vessels/Manifa_35314.

OFF SOMALIA'S EAST COAST [1998]

Sitting on the wooden seat of the houri, Kamil grips the sides as
the inboard motor bounces the boat over the waves toward the reef.
He sees other fishing boats like this one—the small fiberglass craft that
so many Somali fishers use—dotted across the sea, already hauling in
their nets. This morning, Kamil, his father, and two uncles were late
leaving the shore, having spent the early hours mending nets. Yesterday
they'd pulled in more slashed gill nets full of holes, but few tuna.
The damage had become a regular thing.

    Kamil shades his eyes from the glare of sunlight on the water.
He can see the foreign trawlers lurking like hungry sharks far out in the
middle of the rich fishing grounds. Since those trawlers arrived in such
big numbers, it seems that every day of fishing has turned into a battle
for the catch. The trawlers take enormous amounts of tuna, snappers,
sardines, and mackerel, and if that isn't bad enough, they try to keep
local fishers, like Kamil's family, from getting their fair share, often by
vandalizing nets. It was already hard enough to make a living from
these waters, polluted now by unlawful dumping of toxic waste.

    Kamil has heard his father and other fishers on shore talking about
a way to fight against the unfair competition. But it would be a risky
way: piracy. It's easy enough to get guns after so many years of war
in the country. Some fishers who have already turned to piracy are
seizing trawlers at gunpoint, getting quick ransom payments from
owners who don't want anyone to know they are operating illegally.
It seems like an easier way to make money than fishing nowadays.
But Kamil wonders what dangers such a future holds.

The Story of the Sirius Star

Pirate! It's that swashbuckling fellow (or gal) on the deck of a wooden sailing ship, wearing an eye patch, brandishing a cutlass, a parrot perched on his shoulder! You may think of gold coins—pieces of eight—and flags with skull and crossbones. You might not picture a young Somali man in a T-shirt and sarong, wearing sandals or going barefoot. He's holding a submachine gun, riding in an open speedboat.

Even though pirates have been a threat on many of the world's oceans for centuries, today's pirates cut quite a different figure than those storybook characters that first come to mind. But their goals are similar: to loot the ship they capture of its valuables. Except in the 21st century, in the Indian Ocean, the coveted prize is likely to be ransom in US dollars rather than pieces of eight. Who are these modern-day Somali pirates, and why did they risk their lives attacking the *Sirius Star*—one of the largest oil tankers afloat in 2008—off the east coast of Africa?

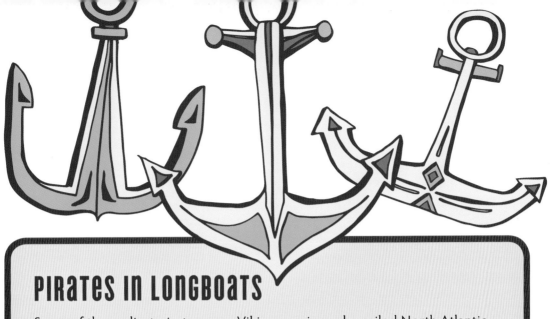

PIRATES IN LONGBOATS

Some of the earliest pirates were Viking warriors who sailed North Atlantic seas from the 8th to 11th centuries. These expert Scandinavian shipbuilders crafted sturdy wooden longboats powered by oars and huge rectangular sails. With a mere 50-centimeter (20-inch) draft, they terrorized merchant ships and villages on shallow coastlines as far east as America. They also raided far inland up rivers in northern Europe, into Russia all the way to the Black Sea, and in the Mediterranean.

Who Will Rule?

A GLIMPSE INTO THE TROUBLED HISTORY of their land offers some answers. The East African country of Somalia juts out into the Indian Ocean and Gulf of Aden, with a coastline of 3,025 kilometers (1,878 miles). On land called the Horn of Africa, it shares borders with Kenya, Ethiopia, and Djibouti. Its capital, Mogadishu, was an Arab settlement in the 10th century and Islam became the main religion. Various European countries controlled the country from the 1800s until 1960, when it gained independence as the United Republic of Somalia. Family groups, or clans, run by warlords then took charge.

But there were constant disagreements over land and borders when Mohamed Siad Barre seized power in 1969 and put a centralized, socialist government in place. Clan rule was forbidden, and banks and businesses were nationalized, or run by the government.

The military dictator's early popularity diminished after 22 years. People felt Barre had become too powerful and his oppressive laws were not applied equally. The clans forced him out in 1991, leaving the country with no stable government to this day. Fighting erupted among the clans, Islamist religious groups, government forces, and neighboring Ethiopian troops. America and the United Nations tried to restore order and distribute food and aid during the civil war, but their intervention failed in the mid-1990s. Now, as various warlords continue to fight for control, the population suffers. People have lost their land, their homes, and jobs. Many have fled as refugees to neighboring countries, and the extreme poverty and starvation are among the worst found anywhere in the world.

Somali children at a refugee camp in 2011

Riches for Some

But Somalia does have something of great value. One
of the richest fisheries in the world exists along its coastline. With no
strong central control or naval patrols to enforce laws, though, foreign
countries began to abuse those ocean resources. Huge trawlers, mainly
from East Asia and Europe, took enormous catches—sometimes cutting
the nets of local fishers, who struggled to make a living. As well, many
countries saw the Somali coast as a good place to get rid of a difficult
and expensive problem: waste. No one would stop them from dumping
radioactive uranium, heavy metals like mercury, and toxic chemical
waste. International governments did not want to get involved in
policing the hundreds of ships working illegally in Somali waters.
Before long, those waters were overfished and dangerously polluted.

A Somali fisher in 2010

In this desperate atmosphere, ordinary Somali fishers tried to protect what belonged to them—their fishing grounds, their main source of income. At gunpoint, they demanded "tax" money from foreign ships to make up for the loss of fish. Some called it "protection for safe passage." The rest of the world called it piracy. Before long, this tactic was more profitable than fishing. Then Somali warlords began to exploit the situation by selling counterfeit licenses to the foreign ships, making huge profits. Little of that money trickled down to the poor.

Encouraged by success with fishing ships, many more fishers eagerly took up the new occupation. Those fishers-turned-pirates seized other fishers' boats to go after foreign emergency aid ships, container ships, oil tankers, and even private yachts. Over 20,000 ships use the Gulf of Aden and sail past Somalia each year, so piracy became big business. The technology used to operate even the largest merchant ships today means that only a small crew is on board, too few to put up any effective resistance against a determined group of pirates. And pirates know their AK-47 submachine guns and rocket-propelled grenade launchers give them the advantage, since laws have prevented commercial ships from carrying weapons.

An 18th-century engraving of pirates Anne Bonny and Mary Read, in their male disguises

NOTORIOUS PIRATES OF THE PAST

The British explorer **SIR FRANCIS DRAKE** took revenge for Spain's attack on his ship by raiding Spanish ships for booty, which he took home to Queen Elizabeth I in England.

WILLIAM KIDD, a Scottish sailor, went to the Indian Ocean to hunt pirates, but became one himself.

English-born **EDWARD TEACH**, better known as the notorious Blackbeard, terrorized Caribbean islands.

Irish-American **ANNE BONNY** disguised herself as a man to plunder Caribbean ships. She married another pirate, the English "Calico Jack" Rackham.

Sirius Star

A Tempting Prize

ONE OF THE BIGGEST CATCHES for the Somali pirates was a supertanker, *Sirius Star*. At 330 meters (1080 feet)—the length of three football fields—it is one of the largest crude oil tankers ever built. It transports oil from Saudi Arabian ports in the Persian Gulf to worldwide markets. But its draft makes it too big to pass through the Suez Canal, the preferred route to reach Europe.

That's why, on November 15, 2008, loaded with 2 million barrels of crude oil bound for Europe, the supertanker was sailing south to go around Africa's Cape of Good Hope. It had reached a point 830 kilometers (450 nautical miles) southeast of Kenya. Once, this distance from the coast would have been enough of a safety margin. In the early 1990s, the small speedboats pirates used could not travel far out to sea. But when pirates began to keep some of the ships they captured, such as fishing trawlers, to serve as "motherships," the situation changed. Motherships are large enough to operate in deep water as bases for smaller open boats. When several of these small boats set off, the mothership stays in contact by satellite phone. It trails a few miles behind, ready to pick up the pirates and any ransom money they collect.

A Fateful Voyage

O<small>N THAT EARLY</small> N<small>OVEMBER MORNING</small>, the crew of the *Sirius Star* was surprised to discover their ship was being shadowed by several small boats. Immediately they put into practice the defense tactics that shipping companies had developed in case of a pirate attack. Security alerts must be sent to naval patrols and to the International Maritime Bureau's Piracy Reporting, which then share the news of attack or capture with law enforcement agencies and alert other ships in the danger zone. Meanwhile, the ship's officer of the watch sounds the whistle, horn, and alarm bells to alert the crew. The pirates attempting to board the vessel will also hear this warning; they'll know they've been seen, and that the crew is preparing to defend the ship. Rolls of razor wire or greased, electrified handrails help prevent attackers from gaining access to a ship.

On an oil carrier the size of the *Sirius Star*, a number of high-pressure fire hoses are placed at intervals on the long decks. Several of the hoses face the stern, the easiest point for the pirates to try to scale the hull with grappling hooks or ladders. If pirates approach the ship, the captain can switch on the hoses from a command post on the bridge. The sight of running hoses might discourage boarding, or the forceful blast of water can knock a pirate off the ladder and prevent him from reaching the deck. Those pirates of old never had to deal with such a weapon!

NAUTICAL TERMS

BEAM: The widest part of a ship

NAUTICAL MILE: 1 nautical mile equals 1.15 land miles, or 1.85 kilometers

DRAFT: The depth a ship's keel (the "backbone" running from front to back along the bottom) reaches below the surface

As the pirates closed in, the captain of *Sirius Star* increased the
ship's speed to 16 knots (about 30 kilometers, or 18 miles, per hour)—
a maximum for a ship of this size. But the faster, lighter pirate boats
overtook the huge vessel, and six armed pirates easily scaled ladders
to the main deck. When huge tankers are fully loaded, their freeboard
(the height of the main deck above the waterline) is relatively short, so
boarding from a small boat is quick and easy. It was too late to reach the
fire hoses, so most of the crew sought refuge in the ship's engine room.
This safe area on many ships can be locked for security, and only those
who know a password or code can get inside. Crew members can secretly
operate the ship from inside the engine room if the captain passes
the control from the bridge. Unfortunately this can only happen for a
short time, as with no visibility from the engine room or navigation
equipment like charts or radar, the ship cannot be safely steered.

Pirates off the coast of Somalia

WHAT IS A "FLAG OF CONVENIENCE"?

Commercial ships must have registration certificates to operate. The flag flown from the ship's stern tells where it is registered. Many shipping companies choose to register their vessels in a country other than their own. Panama and Liberia are two countries that offer what is called a flag of convenience, or FOC, registration. This practice came about after the Second World War in response to US regulations that required all goods shipped between US ports to use US-registered vessels. Shipping companies often found it was less costly to bring goods into the country on foreign ships. While vessels sailing under the Liberian flag are registered in the Liberian port of Monrovia, their main offices may be in the US.

No Escape

DESPITE ALL THE CREW'S EFFORTS, within only 15 minutes, the pirates had taken control of their prize, and their "prisoners of war," as they called them. Further resistance was not worth the risk. Like many in East Africa, pirates chew a narcotic drug known as khat, a stimulant that makes their reactions unpredictable. While ransom money is the first goal of the pirates, and in most cases hostages are unharmed, sometimes violence occurs and captives have been beaten, tortured, and even executed.

The pirates ordered the *Sirius Star* to head closer to the Somali coast. Meanwhile, their ransom demand for 25 million US dollars was sent to the shipping company, with the pirates threatening to harm the crew or sink the ship if their demands were not met.

The prospect of such a huge prize attracted Islamic militias who supported the pirates and wanted a share of the loot. Other groups, though, believed piracy was against Islamic law. Tensions rose, on board but also, with the threat of fighting between these groups, on shore. While the pirates waited for a response to their demand, the ship was moved north of Mogadishu to a pirate base. Because of its size, it had to be held 8 kilometers (5 miles) offshore, in deep water. After the 10-day deadline for payment ran out—without the serious consequences the pirates had threatened—the pirates reduced their price to $10 million. GPS satellites kept track of the ship during further changes of location and negotiations that dragged on for 57 days.

Shipping companies and governments don't want to pay ransoms, which only encourage more piracy. But with hostages' lives at stake, there is little choice. Any attempts to rescue the *Sirius Star* by force, as some local Islamic militia groups opposed to the pirates suggested, were ruled out by the threat of an environmental disaster from spilled oil—the horrendous result if the pirates' bluff became reality.

On January 9, a deal was reached with the shipping company. Parachutes carried the payment, of about $3 million, to the deck of the supertanker. After the pirates had divided up the money, they took off in their small boat for shore. But in rough seas, the overloaded boat capsized, tossing the pirates and their loot overboard. Five men drowned and only three made it to shore, with no money. One body washed up later along with $153,000 in a bag. The pirates' "biggest prize" turned out to be very costly.

A patrol ship watches for pirates on the high seas

The High Price of Piracy

FROM 2007 TO 2013, between 200 and 300 pirates were killed by security forces or lost at sea. But innocent fishers have been mistakenly targeted by security forces as well. While many in Somalia support the pirates' activity and have shared in their cash profits, millions faced with starvation have not fared so well. Even ships bringing food aid from foreign countries have been intercepted, so relief agencies cut back shipments. Amid the political unrest in Somalia, and with money and weapons so plentiful, one of the most serious threats may come from pirate and terrorist groups forming alliances. That could mean the spread of violence beyond local borders.

In a bid to reduce piracy, in 2008 the UN called for a task force of warships and planes to patrol international waters off East Africa. Still, in 2011, Somali pirate hijackings occurred at the rate of one each week. The impact on the shipping world was enormous. Because of sky-high ransoms (totaling up to $385 million per year between 2005 and 2012), insurance costs for shipping ballooned. So did the price tag for additional security—up to $75,000 per trip— after some governments decided to allow armed guards aboard their countries' commercial ships. Egypt's government began to feel the loss of income as fewer companies sent ships through the Suez Canal, choosing instead to send them around the Cape of Good Hope. The longer distance only added to the shipping companies' bills, of course, with an increase in fuel and wages. It also meant longer delivery times for goods—up to an extra three weeks. The price of oil shot up during the 2008 crisis because of the risk to the ship's immense oil cargo. The *Sirius Star* could carry almost a quarter of a day's production from Saudi Arabia's oil fields. The seizure of this ship and others has forced significant changes to commercial shipping.

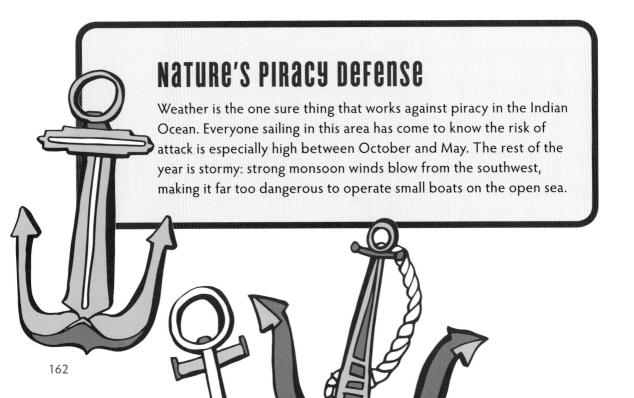

NATURE'S PIRACY DEFENSE

Weather is the one sure thing that works against piracy in the Indian Ocean. Everyone sailing in this area has come to know the risk of attack is especially high between October and May. The rest of the year is stormy: strong monsoon winds blow from the southwest, making it far too dangerous to operate small boats on the open sea.

Somalis wait for water supplies at a refugee camp in 2011

A Better Future?

B<small>Y</small> 2012, <small>PIRATES' SUCCESS BEGAN TO DROP</small> as there were more naval patrols and armed security on merchant ships. But the serious events springing from the small war-torn country of Somalia had finally alerted a world that had largely neglected its troubles. Foreign aid and programs to help rebuild its economy are having an impact. Criminal activity such as selling arms and drugs is ongoing in Somalia, though. Ironically, some pirates who took up arms against ships that were plundering Somalia's fishery resources have found a new occupation: providing paid security (which includes firing on Somali fishers) to those same ships, allowing them to continue their illegal business.

Conclusion

Each of these sea passages involves a particular ship. But it's people who are at the heart of any story about ships. Like the ripples that fan out from a stone dropped in a pond, these stories touched many shores and many lives in diverse ways. They spread knowledge and created new communities. They inspired the development of new technologies and attitudes. They turned some people's lives upside down, and offered unexpected directions to them. They shone a light on inequality in the world. The stories unfold around displays of courage and determination, curiosity and imagination. The greatest legacy of these voyages is in realizing how far the ripples of change traveled when those individual pebbles fell into the oceans of history.

Nowadays, even in the age of air travel, ships continue to play significant roles in our lives. They transport technological equipment and researchers to remote places like Antarctica, and serve as bases of operations. Bulk cargoes of resources such as wood, coal, and oil can still only be moved between continents by ships. Modern fisheries rely on technically advanced ships. We can surf the Internet to learn about distant lands, but nothing compares with a leisurely ocean cruise to tour them.

Once, unfamiliar seas terrified sailors. Today, Earth's vast oceans lure even young people into daring, solo round-the-globe voyages—surely life-changing experiences.

Selected Bibliography

Africa Economic Development Institute. "Pirates of Somalia." *AEDI Exclusives* 1, no. 1
(Mar. 2, 2009). africaecon.org/index.php/exclusives/read_exclusive/1/1.

Anqi, Lu. "Zheng He's Seven Voyages of Peace: An Earlier Era of Oceanic Exploration."
China Pictorial, 2005, no. 7. Retrieved from rmhb.com.cn/chpic/htdocs/english/
content/200507/2-2.htm.

Bond, Larry, ed. *Crash Dive: True Stories of Submarine Combat*. New York: Forge, 2010.

Chaffin, Tom. *The H.L. Hunley: The Secret Hope of the Confederacy*. New York: Hill & Want,
2008.

Cliff, Nigel. *Holy War: How Vasco da Gama's Epic Voyages Turned the Tide in a Centuries-Old
Clash of Civilizations*. New York: HarperCollins, 2011.

Collins, David. *An Account of the English Colony in New South Wales, Vol. 1*. London, 1798;
ebook version Project Gutenberg, 2004. gutenberg.org/files/12565/12565-h/12565-h.htm.

De Quesada, Ricardo Alarcón. "The Long March of the Cuban Revolution." *Monthly
Review: An Independent Socialist Magazine* 60, no. 8 (Jan. 2009): 14–27. Retrieved from
monthlyreview.org/2009/01/01/the-long-march-of-the-cuban-revolution/.

Dower, John. *Black Ships and Samurai*. Massachusetts Institute of Technology Visualizing
Cultures, 2010. ocw.mit.edu/ans7870/21f/21f.027/black_ships_and_samurai/.

Dua, Jatin. "A Pirate's Life for Me." *New Internationalist* 465 (Sept. 2013): 17–19.

First Fleet Fellowship Victoria Inc. "Lady Penrhyn." First Fleet Fellowship Victoria Inc.
website, 2011. firstfleetfellowship.org.au/ships/hms-lady-penrhyn/.

Gruber, Ruth. *Exodus 1947: The Ship That Launched a Nation*. New York: Random House, 1948.

UCLA Center for Chinese Studies. "Zheng He's Voyages of Discovery." UCLA International
Institute website, 2004. international.ucla.edu/china/article/10387.

Immigration Watch Canada. "The Voyage of the Komagata Maru: A Review and Both a
Short and Long Summary." IWC website, May 22, 2008. immigrationwatchcanada.
org/2008/05/22/the-voyage-of-the-komagata-maru-a-review-and-a-short-summary/.

Kapcia, Antoni. *Cuba in Revolution: A History Since the Fifties*. London: Reaktion Books, 2008.

Kazimi, Ali. *Undesirables*. Vancouver: Douglas & McIntyre, 2011.

Keneally, Thomas. *Australians: Origins to Eureka*. Crows Nest, Australia: Allen & Unwin, 2009.

Klinger, Jerry. "In Search of the Exodus." *Jewish Magazine*, Jan. 2010. jewishmag.
com/140mag/exodus/exodus.htm.

"Komagata Maru: Continuing the Journey." Simon Fraser University Library, 2011.
komagatamarujourney.ca/intro.

Levathes, Louise. *When China Ruled the Seas: The Treasure Fleet of the Dragon Throne 1405–1433*.
Toronto: Simon & Schuster, 1994.

Noury, Valerie. "Do Somali Pirates Have Legitimate Grievances?" *New African* 496 (June 2010); 30–31.

Payne, John C. *Piracy Today: Fighting Villainy on the High Seas.* Dobbs Ferry, NY: Sheridan House, 2010.

Phillip, Arthur. *The Voyage of Governor Phillip to Botany Bay, with an Account of the Establishment of the Colonies of Port Jackson and Norfolk Island.* London, 1789.

Phillips, Richard. *A Captain's Duty: Somali Pirates, Navy SEALs and Dangerous Days at Sea.* New York: Hyperion, 2010.

Powell, Eric A. "Hunley Decoded." *Archaeology* 66, no. 3 (May/Jun. 2013): 46–47.

Pringle, Laurence. *The Environmental Movement: From Its Roots to the Challenges of a New Century.* New York: HarperCollins, 2000.

Rennebohm, Max. "Canadians Campaign Against Nuclear Testing on Amchitka Island (Don't Make a Wave), 1969-71." Global Nonviolent Action Database, Dec. 6, 2009. nvdatabase.swarthmore.edu/content/canadians-campaign-against-nuclear-testing-amchitka-island-don-t-make-wave-1969-1971.

Scheele, George A. "Chartered for History: President Warfield to Exodus 1947." Snowden-Warfield Family Geneology Website, 2005. snowden-warfield.com/Stories/CharteredForHistoryPresidentWarfield.htm.

Shimizu, Reiko. *Commodore Matthew Perry: American Black Ships in the Land of the Samurai.* University of Colorado at Boulder, July 26, 2000. willamette.edu/~rloftus/perry.html.

Singh, Rishi. "Canadian Sikh Heritage: The 100 Year History." *Darpan Magazine*, July/August 2007. canadiansikhheritage.ca/en/node/10.

Skierka, Volker. *Fidel Castro: A Biography.* Cambridge: Polity Press, 2004.

Thatcher, Oliver J., ed. "Vasco da Gama: Round Africa to India 1497 to 1498 CE." From The Library of Original Sources (Milwaukee: University Research Extension Co., 1907), Vol. V: 9th to 16th Centuries, 26–40. fordham.edu/halsall/mod/1497degama.asp.

Thomas, Gordon. *Operation Exodus.* New York: St Martin's Press, 2010.

Walworth, Arthur. *Black Ships off Japan: The Story of Commodore Perry's Expedition.* New York: Knopf, 1946.

Watkins, Ronald. *Unknown Seas: How Vasco da Gama Opened the East.* London: John Murray, 2003.

Weyler, Rex. *Greenpeace: How a Group of Ecologists, Journalists and Visionaries Changed the World.* Vancouver: Raincoast Books, 2004.

Further Reading

Bailey, Katherine. *Vasco da Gama: Quest for the Spice Trade*. In the Footsteps of Explorers series. Crabtree, 2007.

Bamberger, David. *Young Person's History of Israel*. Behrman House, 1995.

Blumberg, Rhoda. *Commodore Perry in the Land of the Shogun*. HarperCollins, 2003.

Bowler, Ann Martin. *Adventures of the Treasure Fleet: China Discovers the World*. Tuttle Publishing, 2006.

Bresloff, Robert. *Wanderland*. Diversion Press, 2009.

Connolly, Sean. *Greenpeace*. Smart Apple Media, 2009.

Costain, Meredith. *You Wouldn't Want to Be an 18th-Century British Convict: A Trip to Australia You'd Rather Not Take*. Franklin Watts, 2006.

Dunn, John M., ed. *Modern Day Pirates*. Hot Topics series. Lucent Books, 2011.

Hughes, Susan. *Coming to Canada*. Maple Tree Press, 2005

Jeffrey, Gary. *The Cuban Missile Crisis*. Graphic Modern History: Cold War Conflicts series. Crabtree, 2014.

Johnson, Hugh. *The Voyage of the* Komagata Maru: *The Sikh Challenge to Canada's Colour Bar*. UBC Press, 1989.

Morpurgo, Michael, and Michael Foreman, eds. *Beyond the Rainbow Warrior: A Collection of Stories to Celebrate 25 Years of Greenpeace*. Trafalgar Square, 1997.

Naden, Corinne J. *Fidel Castro and the Cuban Revolution*. World Leaders series. Morgan Reynolds, 2006.

Napoli, Tony. *Vasco da Gama: Discovering the Sea Route to India*. Great Explorers of the World series. Enslow, 2010.

Porterfield, Jason. *Modern-Day Piracy*. In the News series. Rosen Publishing Group, 2010.

Secret Weapon of the Confederacy (DVD). National Geographic. 2013.

Walker, Sally M. *Secrets of a Civil War Submarine: Solving the Mysteries of the H.L. Hunley*. Carolrhoda, 2005.

Yancey, Diane. *Piracy on the High Seas*. World History series. Lucent Books, 2011.

Zullo, Allan. *Escape: Children of the Holocaust*. Scholastic, 2011.

Acknowledgments

I'm grateful to E. Melkumova for floating this idea my way.

With sincere appreciation to Captain A.C. Brooking, Master Mariner, for sharing his expertise and answering my questions about nautical terms and details.

Thanks to everyone at Annick Press for making it such an agreeable experience to contribute another title to the World of Tens series.

Image Credits

Index

G

Germany 80, 105, 106, 107, 112, 126, 131
Global Positioning System (GPS) 25
Granma (newspaper) 119
Greenpeace
    anti-nuclear campaigns 137, 139–40
    campaign to Amchitka 137, 139, 142
    founding 137
    protest tactics 143–44
    Rainbow Warrior ships and 134–35, 140,
        142–45
Guevara, Ernesto (Che) 122–23

H

habeas corpus 94
Haganah (Jewish defense group) 107, 109
head tax 92
Henry the Navigator 25
Hindus 33
Hiroshima and Nagasaki 137
Holocaust 105–8, 112. *See also* refugees
Housatonic, USS 75–76
Hunley, Horace L. 68–69, 74

I

Immigration Act (1910) 90
India 31, 85, 88–91, 96
Indian Ocean 31, 150
Industrial Revolution 43, 66, 135
invasive species 52
Islam 17, 160
Israel 104–6, 113

J

Japan 55, 58–61, 63–66, 69
Jews 101, 105–6, 108–13
July 26 Movement 122

K

Kanagawa Treaty 66
kowtow 10
Kublai Khan 9
Kursk (submarine) 82

L

lead line 29
Leopold, Aldo 138
longboats 151
Lusitania, HMS 71, 80

M

Magellan, Ferdinand 37
Mariel boatlift 128
mariner's astrolabe 28–29
Ming dynasty 9–10
Minamata, Japan 137
Mongols 9
monsoons 31, 34, 162
Moruroa Atoll 140, 142
motherships 156
Muir, John 138
Muslims 26, 31, 33

N

Nanjing, China 5, 13–14, 19
Nautilus (submarine) 79
Navy
    Japanese 67, 80
    Royal Canadian 96
    US 55, 79, 80, 92, 127
Newgate Prison 41, 43–44, 50
North Star 25
nuclear testing 131, 135, 137, 139–40, 142

O

oil spills 137, 142
Order of Christ 27

P

paddle wheels 55, 62, 63
Palestine 105, 107–8, 110, 113
Pearl Harbor attack 92
periscope 78
Perry, Commodore Matthew 55, 63–66
Phillip, Captain Arthur 45, 48, 51
pirates 15, 150–51, 154–62
pollution 135–37, 141–42, 153
Port Jackson 48, 53
Portugal 25–26, 35–37
prison hulks 44

About the Author

GILLIAN RICHARDSON worked as a teacher-librarian in several Canadian provinces before beginning to write her own books. Writing about ships came naturally with several Master Mariners in her seafaring ancestry. Her dad sailed in the British Merchant Navy during the Second World War. Her great-grandfather wrote a navigation manual for young seamen in 1909, and a great-great-grandfather was master of some American and British ships in the late 1800s. Several great-aunts and great-uncles were born at sea around the world. Even with all that salt water in her veins, she still gets seasick, so her favorite view of the ocean is from a beach! She writes—on dry land—at home near Shuswap Lake in British Columbia.

Both of her previous books with Annick Press—*Kaboom! Explosions of All Kinds* and *10 Plants That Shook the World*—are award winners.

About the Illustrator

KIM ROSEN was raised in Pennsylvania, and could usually be found in her room quietly drawing pictures. Kim studied advertising design at the Fashion Institute of Technology in New York City and worked as a designer, then realized she was meant to be an illustrator, and moved to Georgia to attend the Savannah College of Art and Design, where she earned an MFA in illustration.

Today Kim lives with her partner in Northampton, Massachusetts, where she can usually be found in her studio quietly drawing pictures for clients all over the world. She has illustrated for magazines (*The New Yorker*, *The Atlantic*), newspapers (*The Boston Globe*, *The Globe and Mail*) and corporate clients (Billabong, Starbucks, American Express). She is the illustrator of the previous two books in the World of Tens series.

FOR MORE WORLD-CHANGING STORIES, CHECK OUT THESE OTHER BOOKS IN THE WORLD OF TENS SERIES:

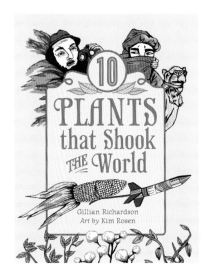 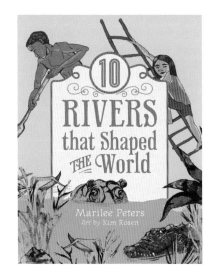

10 PLANTS THAT SHOOK THE WORLD
Gillian Richardson, illustrated by Kim Rosen
PAPERBACK $14.95 HARDCOVER $24.95

✷ *Eureka Honor Award, California Reading Association*
✷ *Best Books for Kids and Teens 2013, starred selection, Canadian Children's Book Centre*

"An intriguing and well-designed study of the ways plants have helped start wars, cure diseases, and advance technology."
—*Publishers Weekly*, starred review

"Readers who took these plants for granted before may well not do so anymore."
—*Kirkus Reviews*

10 RIVERS THAT SHAPED THE WORLD
Marilee Peters, illustrated by Kim Rosen
PAPERBACK $14.95 HARDCOVER $24.95

Rivers can make civilizations rise or crumble, divide cultures or link them together, and even provide crucial clues to where we came from. Dive into these 10 stories about the surprising power of rivers through the ages.